# GET
### THE
# TRUTH

## ALSO BY PHILIP HOUSTON, MICHAEL FLOYD, AND SUSAN CARNICERO

*Spy the Lie*

# GET
## THE
# TRUTH

## FORMER CIA OFFICERS TEACH YOU HOW TO PERSUADE ANYONE TO TELL ALL

PHILIP HOUSTON, MICHAEL FLOYD
AND SUSAN CARNICERO

Commentary by PETER ROMARY

Written by DON TENNANT

ICON

Previously published in the UK in 2015
by Icon Books Ltd

This edition published in the UK in 2016
by Icon Books Ltd, Omnibus Business Centre,
39–41 North Road, London N7 9DP
email: info@iconbooks.com
www.iconbooks.com

First published in the USA in 2015
by St Martin's Press, Press, 175 Fifth Avenue,
New York, N.Y. 10010

Sold in the UK, Europe and Asia
by Faber & Faber Ltd, Bloomsbury House,
74–77 Great Russell Street,
London WC1B 3DA or their agents

Distributed in the UK, Europe and Asia
by TBS Ltd, TBS Distribution Centre, Colchester Road,
Frating Green, Colchester CO7 7DW

Distributed in Australia and New Zealand
by Allen & Unwin Pty Ltd,
PO Box 8500, 83 Alexander Street,
Crows Nest, NSW 2065

Distributed in South Africa by
Jonathan Ball, Office B4, The District,
41 Sir Lowry Road, Woodstock 7925

Distributed in India by Penguin Books India,
7th Floor, Infinity Tower – C, DLF Cyber City,
Gurgaon 122002, Haryana

ISBN: 978-178578-029-5

Designed by Steven Seighman

Printed and bound in the UK by Clays Ltd, St Ives plc

*For all whose pursuit of the truth*
*keeps us safe*

# CONTENTS
||||||||||||||||||||

# PREFACE

|||||||||||||

It's still dark out—the sun won't rise for another couple of hours. You're standing in front of a heavily secured door that opens to a small, musty, windowless room in a nondescript building at a secret location outside the United States. On the other side of the door is a man who had been brought to the room several hours earlier, after a clandestine operation executed by U.S. military forces and intelligence operatives led to his capture. This man may have been involved in orchestrating the September 11 attacks that had changed life as you and the rest of the Western world had known it.

The man, classified by the U.S. government as a "high value detainee," won that distinction for a reason: The knowledge he possesses could be a treasure trove of information not only about the planning and execution of the September 11 attacks, but potentially about other attacks, possibly even more heinous, that are being plotted. At this moment, there is no higher priority in the War on Terror than extracting that information from this man. The lives of what could be thousands, or even tens of thousands, of innocent people—men, women, and children—could hang in the balance. Your job is to get the man to tell you everything he knows. It's difficult to conceive of a more daunting task, with as much at stake. What approach, what techniques, give you the best possible chance of succeeding when you walk through that door?

This book will answer that question.

At its core, it's a book about influence. It's about the process of exerting influence to elicit truthful information from a person who has a reason—not uncommonly, a reason that involves life-altering consequences—to want to withhold that information. Some of the techniques that in recent years have been associated with this process have sparked an intense, emotional debate in the United States and around the world. It's especially intense and emotional when the discussion focuses on the organization to which we have largely dedicated our careers, and indeed much of our lives: the Central Intelligence Agency.

In our world, the process is commonly referred to as *interrogation*. Of course, it's difficult to mention interrogation and the CIA in the same sentence without readily conjuring up preconceived notions, and disturbing mental images, of what the process must entail in our high-stakes world of counterespionage and counterterrorism. Such preconceptions can easily be forgiven, because there has been more than sufficient public disclosure of methods that have been employed since the War on Terror was declared on September 11, 2001, to substantiate the conclusions that many have legitimately drawn. "Enhanced interrogation techniques" is the euphemism of choice among its proponents. But it remains exactly that: a euphemism.

Sometimes, when the task at hand is to describe what something is, it's helpful to describe what it isn't. This book is not a position paper on interrogation techniques employed by the Central Intelligence Agency, or any other agency or institution. It is not a vehicle for the delivery of an argument, nor an apology for anything that anyone sees as warranting an apology, nor is it an attempt to stifle any debate. But to the extent that the debate will continue over the interrogation techniques that we as a nation should be prepared to employ in the interest of protecting our national security, it is a debate that will continue outside these pages. Simply put, that's not our call.

All we can do is speak from our own experiences, drawn from careers that, in essence, were built around a single, quantifiable, yet extraordinarily challenging goal: getting people to tell the truth. We've pursued that goal for decades, along career paths that intersected in a way that has enabled us to learn from each other, and to meld our individual experiences into a comprehensive, cohesive body of work. It is upon that body of work that our activities as a team, and specifically our methodology for getting to the truth, have been established.

Perhaps the creation and sophistication of that methodology can best be described as a team sport, with Phil Houston acting as the player-coach. Phil, who served in senior positions within the Office of Security during the course of his twenty-five years at the Agency, is widely considered by his peers, and by some senior officials in the U.S. government, to be among the best interrogators the CIA has ever had. Indeed, his track record includes successes in some of the highest-profile cases in the Agency's history. Michael Floyd, meanwhile, parlayed his experience and reputation as one of the nation's foremost polygraph authorities to become a key resource in the fields of interviewing and interrogation not only in the CIA, but in the National Security Agency, as well. Susan Carnicero's CIA career began as an operative under deep cover in the Agency's Directorate of Operations, now known as the National Clandestine Service. Susan's unique skill set, including her expertise in criminal psychology, would prove to be an invaluable asset in establishing her as one of the Agency's most accomplished interrogators and screening specialists.

Our team was, to be sure, a formidable one. And smart enough to draft an ideal new player when the opportunity arose. That new player is Peter Romary, a seasoned trial attorney, educator, and internationally recognized expert in mediation and negotiation. Peter has devoted his career to service that is ultimately best encapsulated as pursuing the same goal as that of the rest of the team: getting people to tell the truth. With the team in place, then, the story of what we do and how we do it, and of how it can be practiced by anyone in any situation that involves eliciting truthful information from someone else, can be fully shared.

We took a similar tack in our previous book, *Spy the Lie: Former CIA Officers Teach You How to Detect Deception*, authored by the original trio of Phil, Michael, and Susan. In that book, we shared our methodology for determining whether or not someone is lying, and showed how it can be applied in everyday life. Those skills, as immensely valuable as they are, constitute a separate set of tools that need not be acquired in order to understand and apply our methodology for getting someone to tell you the truth. In other words, while it would be helpful, reading *Spy the Lie* is not a prerequisite for reading *Get the Truth*. That said, readers of *Spy the Lie* will recognize several familiar characters when they read this book. In that book, we showed how we determined that those characters were lying. In this one, the stories will revolve around how we got them to tell us the truth.

There's another connection that's worth mentioning. In *Spy the Lie*, we dispelled quite a few myths, and challenged widespread presumptions, that have long been relied upon to spot deception. In short, we shared our own real-life experiences, which have shown that a lot of the techniques people rely upon to determine whether someone is lying simply aren't as reliable as they would have us believe. The interrogation methodology we will share in this book may come as an even more surprising challenge to conventional wisdom. In the minds of many, interrogation, almost by definition, is a harsh, confrontational encounter. In truth, that's more likely to define a *failed* interrogation. Perhaps an apt analogy is the difference between war and diplomacy: You can seek your objective by means of trampling the enemy, or you can opt instead for the art of negotiation and influence. We've found the latter option to be overwhelmingly more effective.

Over the years, we've had to defend that position under some pretty intense circumstances. But there's one thing we've never had to do: We've never had to come up with a socially or politically palatable euphemism for what it is we're engaged in. The following pages will explain why. More important, they will explain *how* what we do can be adapted, with remarkable effectiveness, by anyone, in any capacity, whose aim is to get the truth.

I do not like that man. I must get to know him better.

—ABRAHAM LINCOLN

# 1.

# OF ESPIONAGE AND INFOMERCIALS: THE EXTRAORDINARY POWER OF SHORT-TERM THINKING

||||||||||||||||||||||||||||||||||||||||||||||||||||||

The headquarters of the Central Intelligence Agency in Langley, Virginia, has changed a lot over the years. But the original headquarters building, designed in the 1950s by the same New York architectural firm that designed the United Nations building in New York, is a massive concrete structure that hadn't changed much at all by the early 1980s, when Phil Houston began his assignment as a polygraph examiner in the Office of Security's Polygraph Division. The compartmented nature of the work of the CIA meant that few employees had routine access to any work area in the building beyond their own departments, so there was only one work area in which virtually all employees would have occasion to find themselves at one time or another. That area was the Polygraph Division.

The workload of the Agency's polygraph examiners was, as a natural consequence, consistently heavy. Between the screening of job applicants, the routine reinvestigation of Agency employees, and the occasional investigation of alleged improper or criminal conduct, the days had precious little downtime.

For Phil, the pace was as exhilarating as the work itself. A relatively junior employee in those early years, he was finding that despite his lack of tenure he was getting good at this stuff, and he loved the opportunity that each encounter provided to hone his skills. He welcomed the assignment he received one morning to conduct a routine reinvestigation of a CIA employee we'll call "Mary," just as he did every other assignment that came his way. There appeared to be nothing out of the ordinary in this particular case, but that was okay. Phil recognized that handling the run-of-the-mill cases was part of the job.

Mary was a midlevel manager who had spent at least one tour overseas, a somewhat plain woman who had never been married, and who had likely turned few heads in her travels. She had been through the polygraph drill before, so she was familiar with the process, and seemed comfortable as Phil began running through the standard list of questions in the pretest. But any comfort she was feeling was short-lived. When Phil got to the requisite question about whether she had ever worked for a foreign intelligence service, Mary's behavior indicated that the question troubled her for some reason. Sure enough, when Phil asked her the question during the polygraph examination, it was clear there was an issue.

It was equally clear that if there was one issue that required immediate resolution, it was a bad response to the "have you ever worked for the bad guys" question. As critical as the situation was, Phil's sense was that whatever was causing Mary's concern with the question was unlikely to be anything monumental. After all, Mary appeared to fit the mold of a reserved spinster much more readily than that of a cloak-and-dagger temptress. In his naturally low-key, easygoing, North Carolinian style, Phil began the process of getting to the root of the problem.

"Mary, this happens all the time with people we talk to,

because they'll have something in their mind that's no big deal, but, for any number of reasons, the more they think about it, the more they're bothered by it," Phil assured her. "Sometimes it's just a harmless oversight, sometimes it's just a minor lapse in judgment that we blow out of proportion because we're so concerned about doing the right thing."

Mary nodded.

"I think that's it. There was a security violation," she said. Mary went on to explain that during her recent overseas tour, she had used government resources to do an unauthorized favor for one of the locals. After she recounted the details of the incident, Phil was relieved. No doubt, what Mary had done was a blatant violation of regulations. But Phil knew it happens far more frequently than U.S. government employees working overseas would care to admit. Still, the matter needed to be fully resolved.

"I understand," Phil nodded consolingly. "You're not the first one to do that." He smiled. "Let's talk about it so we can get it completely off your chest, okay? Was this local an acquaintance of yours?"

Yes, he was an acquaintance, Mary said. And there was more. Much more. The conversation led to a series of admissions that would leave Phil stunned. This acquaintance, whom we'll call "Charmer," happened to work for the local government. As the interview progressed, Mary confided to Phil that Charmer, in fact, worked for the local government as an intelligence officer. The revelations became steadily more serious as the hours passed. By the end of the second day, Mary had admitted that she and Charmer had become romantically involved.

Phil now recognized that he was sitting across from a midlevel CIA manager who had been in bed with a foreign intelligence officer. What might she have shared with Charmer during their intimate moments? Phil knew it was essential to get Mary to share anything that she might have divulged to Charmer. Mary's embarrassment by that point was obvious, and she was crying. Phil did his best to make it as painless for her as he could.

"Mary," Phil said gently, "let's not lose sight of what we're dealing with here. It's not like you're a spy. It's not like you gave him everything. If there was some pillow talk, we just need to talk about it so we can clear this up."

Suddenly, Mary stopped crying, and she looked up. "Phil, you don't understand," she whispered. "I *did* give him everything."

Those words hit Phil squarely in the gut, instantly evoking a mix of emotions that must be close to what a first responder feels when he arrives at the scene of some tragic event. As the enormity of the task at hand presents itself, instinct takes over, emotions are pushed aside, and the safety and security of others becomes paramount. In Phil's job, it was a matter of tapping what psychologists call *ideational fluency*—the ability to shift one's thinking instantaneously as the situation warrants. Phil's fluency seemed inborn.

"Okay, well, let's talk about that," Phil said. He began what would be several days of debriefing, and the admissions from Mary spilled unabated into the open. She had indeed given Charmer the whole works. She had identified every station officer. She had disclosed every operation. She had taken and handed over photos of the entire station complex. And she had passed along the identities and photos of every human asset she was aware of. There was only one word for the activity she had engaged in: espionage.

In all, Phil spent eight days working with Mary. One of those days was spent on the question of what Charmer had given her in return for the information. Mary admitted to receiving "a few pieces of jewelry" from him, but would go no further. She failed the polygraph on the question of additional compensation.

The Agency's counterintelligence team was kept fully briefed throughout the process, as was the FBI. As Phil spoke with Mary, dots were being connected in the background. Although Mary never admitted it, Charmer, it turned out, wasn't just working for the local intelligence operation. He was an agent for the hostile intelligence service of another foreign government. And it got worse. During Mary's assignment at that overseas location, one of the Agency's assets there had been killed. The Agency had no doubt that the killing was intelligence-related, but no one at the time could figure out how the operation had been compromised. Mary admitted to Phil that that was one of the operations she had disclosed to Charmer.

Phil hated Mary for that. Whether those feelings were right or wrong, when Phil learned of her betrayal—not just of the Agency, but of every man, woman, and child in the country—he absolutely despised Mary. Yet as the debriefing continued, Phil's gentleness never faltered. At the end of the eighth day, when it was all over, Mary approached Phil, and hugged him.

"Thank you, Phil," she said. "Thank you for understanding."


The enormity of the case was lost on no one at the FBI, least of all the Bureau's assistant director for intelligence. The day after Mary admitted that she had given "everything" to Charmer, the assistant director was in the office of William Kotapish, the CIA's director of security, being briefed by Phil. When Phil recounted what Mary had admitted to having passed to Charmer, the FBI assistant director was ready to take over what he saw as a clear-cut espionage case. A senior

Agency counterintelligence officer, who was also in the meeting, chimed in that Phil's debriefing of Mary was ongoing.

"For whatever reason, she likes talking to him," the counterintelligence officer said. Phil didn't appreciate the slight, lowly employee or not. "Hey, I can hear you," he muttered to himself. It was hardly a matter of Mary liking her conversations with Phil. It was that Phil had followed a meticulously choreographed process to get her to that point.

The counterintelligence officer proclaimed that another issue stood in the way of the Bureau taking over the case: The admissions that Phil had elicited from Mary were classified. And declassifying any of it was out of the question.

Kotapish suggested the Bureau conduct its own investigation, a suggestion the FBI assistant director readily embraced. He picked up the gray line—the secure telephone line linking government agencies—and called the Bureau's Washington field office. He arranged for two FBI agents to interview Mary at her home that evening.

As it turned out, the FBI's investigation was over almost before it began. The two agents who interviewed Mary got nowhere. It was probably the worst of all possible outcomes: Yes, she told the Agency all of those things, Mary said. But she had made it all up. None of it was true. She agreed to a polygraph examination by the Bureau, and, naturally, she failed it. But with no evidence against her, and with the Agency unable to declassify the information Phil had elicited from her, the Bureau had no choice but to cut Mary loose.

When Phil learned of that outcome, he was very much aware of what had gone wrong. He had worked tirelessly to keep Mary firmly in what we call "short-term thinking mode." That is, he interacted with her in a way that kept her focused where he wanted her. He had kept the number of factors in her decision making as narrow, and as immediate, as he possibly could. When Mary spoke with the two FBI agents, those decision-making factors expanded dramatically, and were radically reprioritized. She had switched into long-term thinking mode. Now, other factors were influencing her—like the prospect of prison and the end of life as she knew it.

The way it all played out can't be disclosed, but we can share one dimension of the outcome. One evening during that eight-day span, Phil was at home, and the phone rang. It was the Agency's Security Duty Office.

"Phil, do you know a woman by the name of Mary Smith?" the officer asked. Phil said he did, and the officer continued.

"She called us a little while ago and claimed that she has been in a polygraph conversation with you, and that we should call you. She said she had left some valuables in the ladies' restroom this afternoon before she left the building. She said to call you, and you would authorize us to release it to her."

The officer went on to explain that he had gone up to retrieve the valuables, which turned out to be a large bag of jewelry. He said Mary told him that she had been keeping the bag in her safe at work because some of it was extremely valuable, and she felt it would be safer there. Phil got in touch with Bill Kotapish, the director of security, and filled him in. The two agreed that most, if not all, of the jewelry was likely the booty she had received from Charmer, and that now she wanted to hide it. In the end, there was no need. The CIA's Office of the General Counsel determined that the Agency had no right to confiscate it. The jewelry was returned to Mary.

For Phil, Mary's case was by no means the total debacle it might have been. Through it, he gained insights that would serve him and others in the Agency and beyond extremely well in the years that followed. Perhaps most significantly, it helped to crystallize a concept that would be a critical underpinning of our interrogation methodology: the psychology of short-term thinking.

To fully appreciate the power—and the ubiquity—of the concept, consider a contrivance that most of us probably see more frequently than we might acknowledge, or perhaps even realize: the infomercial.

Almost all of us have watched our fair share of them—earnest, often unapologetically kitschy productions, touting products we never knew we needed, from blankets with sleeves to weights you shake. Why do these pitches work? Why do so many people find themselves picking up the phone to buy a little putting green to use while sitting on the toilet? The reason is that these marketers take full advantage of the psychology of short-term thinking to influence our decision making in a way that compels us to do what they want us to do—buy a product that we wouldn't necessarily be inclined to buy.

To accomplish that, the marketers capitalize on four factors that propel us into short-term thinking mode: our inherent vulnerability to influence; repetition; loss of independent thinking; and a lack of immediately identifiable consequences. Let's take a look at how that works.

### Inherent vulnerability to influence

When we're watching an infomercial, we're at a disadvantage in that there's a one-way flow of information. We have no means of asking any questions or challenging any claims. Consequently, the marketer's message is our sole source of data upon which to base our decision.

### Repetition

It's a psychological truism that the higher the number of instances we hear something, the greater the likelihood we'll accept it, or at least open the door to the possibility of accepting it. A fundamental characteristic of infomercials is the repetition of visual imagery that illustrates application of the product under various circumstances, or by various individuals.

## Loss of independent thinking

How frequently do you make the conscious decision to turn on the TV for the purpose of watching an infomercial so you can purchase a product you've never even heard of? Probably not all that frequently. The very act of viewing the infomercial is one that likely wasn't actively chosen of your own accord.

## Lack of immediately identifiable consequences

There's a reason why these marketers don't tell you to take out your checkbook, or to get your credit card number handy. All they ask you to do is make a telephone call. What harm is there in that? In fact, if you call in the next ten minutes, they'll double the offer! Where's the downside?

What's happening here is that you have any number of reasons why you wouldn't want to buy, say, a pair of plastic sandals with built-in exfoliating brushes. But you're introduced to multiple reasons why you *might* be interested in buying them. The marketers are working to make the reasons you wouldn't want to buy them go away, or to at least reprioritize them so that the reasons you might want to buy them go up on top. Before you know it, you have a snazzy new pair of plastic exfoliating sandals sitting in your closet.

Successfully bringing those four factors to bear compels people to do whatever it is we want them to do. It involves temporarily replacing the factors they're inclined to focus on

## SHORT-TERM THINKING: FOUR FACTORS

- Inherent vulnerability to influence
- Repetition
- Loss of independent thinking
- Lack of immediately identifiable consequences

with those we want them to focus on, or to at least reprioritize them so the ones we want them to focus on are on top. That's the concept of short-term thinking. We tap the very same principle in any interrogation scenario we encounter, whether the aim is to get a terrorist to disclose the details of a bomb plot, a serial killer to confess to a murder, a job applicant to share his drug-related indiscretions, or a child to admit she didn't do her homework.

# 2.

# THE BEST-CASE/
# WORST-CASE CONTINUUM

||||||||||||||||||||||||||||||||||||||||||||||||||||||

They say sometimes it's better to be lucky than good. They're probably right.

The moment Mary dropped the bombshell in that interview with Phil that she had had a romantic relationship with a man who was working as a foreign intelligence officer, everything changed. With that admission, the situation Phil confronted became a matter of urgent concern. In the position she held at that overseas location, Mary had access to information that, if disclosed to a hostile intelligence service, would cause irreparable harm to the United States' interests there, and would put the lives of individuals loyal to the United States in imminent danger. If Mary had shared any classified information at all with Charmer, it was absolutely essential that the Agency know, so it could determine what might have been compromised. Phil instantly set out on that quest.

Reacting to Mary's startling revelation in a harsh or adversarial manner, Phil well knew, would thwart his chances of getting that information, since it would almost certainly cause Mary to throw up her defenses, or even to shut down. The stakes were too high. Mary could easily have said something she shouldn't have said in an intimate moment, and Phil needed Mary to be willing to open up to him.

"Mary, let's not lose sight of what we're dealing with here," Phil said, as you may recall. "It's not like you're a spy. It's not like you gave him everything. If there was some pillow talk, we just need to talk about it so we can clear this up."

You may also recall Mary's response: "Phil, you don't understand. I *did* give him everything."

Call it providential. Call it sheer luck. Whatever it was, it was very, very fortunate. Because the route Phil was taking could easily have ended in a catastrophic derailment.

What if Mary had heard what Phil said, and had the presence of mind to capitalize on it? Suppose that instead of the way it actually went, it had gone something like this:

"When you said that, Phil, it made me think. Could I have said something at some point when we were lounging in bed with a bottle of wine? We did talk about our workdays in very general terms sometimes, just things like how crazy the day was, or that I had to work later than usual. I honestly don't think I ever said anything to him that mattered, Phil. I hope to God I never said anything that mattered."

No doubt, Phil could have worked with that response, and ultimately might well have gotten to the same place: an admission from Mary that she had given Charmer everything. But he might have been beaten. And if he had been, despite giving it his best shot, the reason would have been readily apparent: When it really counted, his aim was way too low.

To understand the target, think of a continuum that represents Mary's actions. On one end of the continuum is the best-case scenario; on the other, the worst-case scenario. In Phil's interview with Mary, the best-case scenario was probably that she was guilty of some serious indiscretions and that she had violated a trust by knowingly engaging in a relationship with a foreign intelligence officer, but no classified information had been compromised. The worst-case scenario was that she had been recruited by a foreign intelligence service, and that she had actively engaged in espionage against the United States.

When Mary admitted to Phil that she had been in a romantic relationship with Charmer, Phil's assumption was that this lonely woman had simply allowed her heart to rule her head—that she had exercised exceedingly poor judgment, but with no real intent to cause any harm. Still, recognizing that people let their guard down and become more open in such circumstances, Phil was well aware of the urgency of the matter. He saw the immediate task at hand as determining what Mary might have said to Charmer in those unguarded moments.

Phil had pegged Mary's activity very close to the "best-case" end of the continuum, without sufficient evidence to do so. That misreading led to the "pillow talk" question.

Mary's confession would ultimately pinpoint where she really was on the continuum—as it turned out, she was squarely on the opposite end. Phil had missed it by a mile.

He vowed to never let that happen again.


At an overseas location about a year later, Phil was studiously reviewing a case file. He had been dispatched to the region to conduct security interviews with several foreign assets—individuals who had been recruited to serve as intelligence operatives. It was a routine procedure that these operatives were required to undergo on a fairly regular basis, just as Agency employees themselves underwent periodic security reinvestigations. The case Phil was reviewing was that of a foreign asset we'll call "Omar," a high-value, trusted local who had served the Agency well over the course of twenty years since he had been recruited. Omar's record was impressive.

Phil had reviewed the case files of dozens of assets all over the world, and it was easy to see why this guy stood out as an especially highly prized source. Beyond all that, no areas of concern had arisen in Omar's previous security interviews. So when Phil closed the file and left his secure location for the meeting, he was confident this one would be a breeze. Two hours, tops, and then he'd be able to meet up with a co-worker to get some dinner.

The prearranged meeting place was a high-rise hotel in the center of the city. A suite on one of the higher floors had been secured for the interview, and when Omar showed up, Phil's colleagues confirmed that the hookup had gone as planned—no signs of any surveillance. Phil greeted Omar with a friendly handshake, and the two exchanged a few pleasantries. Thankfully, Omar's English was strong—there would be no need for an interpreter, which was always a welcome discovery. Interviewing an asset through a third party was certainly doable—we do it all the time—but it was suboptimal, at best. Too many times, we'll ask a question during an interview of a non-English speaker, he'll respond with what sounds like a lengthy diatribe, and the interpreter will turn to us and say something like, "Not really." Determining what was lost in translation is always an adventure.

Phil and Omar made themselves comfortable in the sitting area of the suite. Phil got straight to work, methodically covering the prepared list of standard questions. It was all going as painlessly as Phil expected it would. And then he got to the question about whether Omar had ever worked for a foreign intelligence service.

"Omar, you've worked with us for years," Phil said. "Have you ever worked with anybody else?"

There was a pause. Omar seemed to be gathering his thoughts as he shifted in his seat. He finally voiced his response.

"Can I pray?"

Another pause. *Can you pray? What on earth do you mean, can you pray?* Phil was scrambling to figure out what to make of the request. He was determined not to let his bewilderment show.

"Sure, no problem," Phil said matter-of-factly, as if a prayer break was a typical element of his interviews. With instinctive reverence, given his Catholic upbringing, Phil found himself lowering his head slightly, but with his eyes squarely on Omar. He expected to see Omar bowing his head in prayer. Instead, he saw Omar rise from his chair and walk into the bathroom.

A moment later, Omar emerged with a towel, and walked toward the window in the sitting area. If he didn't know better, Phil would have thought his colleagues from the local operation were pranking him. He was struggling to make some sense of Omar's actions, but to no avail.

*What is this guy doing?* Phil's mind was racing. *Is he going to try to signal somebody with the towel? How bad is this going to get?*

As Omar unfolded the towel and gazed out the window, Phil suddenly remembered. Omar, a Muslim, was getting his bearings so he could face Mecca as he prayed. He spread the towel on the floor and prostrated himself on it. After about ten minutes of silent prayer, Omar arose, returned to his seat, and thanked Phil for accommodating his request.

"Of course," Phil said. He asked Omar if he was ready to resume. Omar nodded.

"Okay," Phil said. "Omar, have you ever worked for any other intelligence service?" Phil's voice was just as relaxed as it had been earlier, perhaps just a bit quieter.

Omar looked at Phil. Again, he appeared to be conducting a mental search. Shifting his feet uneasily and dabbing the perspiration from his brow, he responded.

"Sir, why are you asking me this? Is there a concern?"

If ever there was a loaded word in the English language, it's *interrogation*. It's a word that stirs emotions and creates uneasiness. And for good reason. In the contexts that we most commonly hear and read it, the word evokes images of intense verbal abuse, even physical violence. It's understood as being harsh, intimidating, often threatening. Consequently, we've found that in our discussion of the topic, we need to precede the word with a modifier to identify the form of interrogation to which we subscribe, the one that is most likely to result in a successful outcome: *noncoercive*. We should point out, moreover, that we use the word *elicitation* interchangeably with *interrogation*. All of this begs an obvious question: Regardless of what you call it, what is it?

The idea is pretty simple: Think of it as a process that's designed to influence or persuade an individual to reveal information that he has reason to want to conceal. So what's the difference between that and interviewing? Interviewing is a means of collecting from a person information that he has no reason to want to withhold. There's another distinction that may not be as readily comprehensible: An interview is a dialogue. An interrogation, counterintuitive as it may seem, is a monologue.

As distinct as the two processes are, shifting from interview mode to interrogation mode needs to be accomplished seamlessly, imperceptibly. No doubt, Omar never recognized the switch.

Up until the point just after Omar paused to pray, when Phil repeated the question about whether Omar had ever worked for another intelligence service, Phil was squarely in interview mode. He had no reason up to that point to believe there was anything Omar felt compelled to conceal. That changed the moment Phil heard Omar's response:

"Sir, why are you asking me this? Is there a concern?"

That behavior told Phil that Omar had a problem with the question—that there was something on his mind that he didn't want to disclose. Phil's task was to find out what that something was. Time to retrieve the best-case/worst-case continuum.

The best-case scenario, as Phil saw it, was that the question caused something relatively innocuous to pop into Omar's mind. Perhaps he had been approached by someone he suspected of working for a foreign intelligence service, but failed to report it. Perhaps he had a friend or a relative with connections to a foreign intelligence service, and he never disclosed it. The worst-case scenario was chilling, given the ramifications: Omar was a double agent, and was actively engaged in espionage against the United States.

So where on the continuum did Omar's problematic information likely lie? What facts did Phil have at his disposal upon which to base a decision? He knew that Omar had been a highly regarded asset for two decades, one upon whom Phil's in-country colleagues had relied heavily in developing and executing key intelligence operations. He knew that Omar had undergone security reviews just like this one at regular intervals over the years, and that he had passed every one with flying colors. Phil had every reason to peg Omar on the best-case end of the continuum, did he not?

Perhaps he did. But as Phil sat in that hotel suite looking at Omar and assimilating his response, the memory of how he had been burned in Mary's case flashed before him.

Never again.

"Omar, there's clearly something here that you're not telling me, that we need to talk about," Phil said, his voice unrushed, his tone unruffled. Omar said nothing. Phil continued.

"Listen, I know how loyal you've been to us. We all know that, Omar. Our guys here talk about you with genuine admiration because of the help you've provided all these years. One guy told me he trusts you like he trusts his own family. *Like his own family.* I don't think I've ever heard anyone I've worked with say that about anybody else. It's a remarkable thing. So please don't think I'm not fully aware of what you mean to this operation. I am. But I also know that sometimes things just happen, Omar. They just happen. Everybody's in that boat. It's just the way life is. And everybody knows that, Omar. You're one of the good guys, but stuff happens to good guys, too. So whatever it is you're worried about, we just need to talk about it so we can fix it and move on. There's too much important work to do to get bogged down in something that's not necessarily anybody's fault. Whatever it is that you're concerned about telling me is fixable. What is it, Omar?"

By that point, the interview was entering its third hour. Phil remained patient. Omar stared distantly, as if trying to recall something. He shook his head, not in denial, but as if he was unable to remember. He looked at Phil.

"I don't know," Omar said, still appearing to be deep in thought. "I don't know anyone who works for another intelligence service."

It was an interesting response—interesting for its specificity. Phil hadn't asked Omar whether he knew anyone who worked for another intelligence service. He simply asked what it was that Omar was concerned about telling him. It got more interesting. Much more interesting.

"Okay," Phil said. Omar continued to shake his head, his expression pensive.

Then, it happened. Omar made a mistake. Without realizing it, he betrayed himself.

"No," Omar said, sounding more decisive. "No, I don't know any Menacians." (*Authors' note: Due to the sensitivity of the matter, the foreign country involved can't be disclosed. We'll re-*

*fer to it here by the fictitious name,* Menacia, *and to its citizens as* Menacians.)

Bingo. The statement created an odd mix of exhilaration and apprehension within Phil. On the one hand, in hearing those words, he knew he had made a quantum leap in getting to the truth. On the other, the truth was looking manifestly ominous. Omar had just conveyed a quintessential example of what we call an "unintended message," or what we sometimes refer to as "truth in the lie." We've seen it time and time again: Without realizing it, deceptive people often convey a revealing message in the words they choose to articulate the lie. And the message in this case was sobering: This longtime, trusted asset at minimum had a Menacian connection.

Phil didn't miss a beat. He resumed his monologue, but with a subtle shift. His general, "there's something we need to talk about" approach needed to be narrowed.

"I understand, Omar. In this job, we meet so many people from so many different backgrounds, under so many different kinds of circumstances, that sometimes it's really difficult to keep track of who's who. My wife will tell you, I'll meet one of her friends one week, and the next week she'll mention the friend, and I'll have no idea who she's talking about. Okay, shame on me, but my wife doesn't realize how many people we meet in this line of work."

Omar was nodding appreciatively, as if thinking about his own wife. Phil continued.

"Hey, I've met Menacians, I've met Chinese, I've met people from all over—that's the nature of the work we do. I can't imagine that it wouldn't be the same way with you. So just because you might have met a Menacian at some point doesn't mean there's a problem, Omar. It just means we need to disclose that so that everything's done by the book and there are no misunderstandings."

You get the drift. After a few more minutes, Phil paused to determine where Omar's head was by that point. It was in a different place. Omar was starting to remember. Yes, he had met a Menacian. But it was a long time ago—more than twenty years ago. Yes, Omar acknowledged, the Menacian worked for his country's intelligence service. And yes, the Menacian had tried to recruit him. Before long, Omar delivered the coup de grâce: Yes, the Menacian had been successful.

Phil reacted as if Omar had just told him that although he had sworn himself to vegetarianism twenty years ago, he had been eating cheeseburgers all along. As Omar's stream of admissions continued to flow, he soon fell off the worst-case end of the continuum. Omar had been recruited by the Menacian Intelligence Service (MIS) all those years ago for a very specific mission: to operate as a double agent against the CIA.

Now the scope of Phil's monologue had narrowed again. He had to find out as much as he could about Omar's mission, and what he had passed to the Menacians.

"Omar, listen," Phil said, as composed as he had been from the outset. "We can't change history. But that's what it is, Omar—it's history. Whatever the Menacians have asked you to do, we can't undo that. You can't change it, and I can't change it. All we can do to salvage this situation is to figure out what we're going to do from here—what's our best course of action."

Omar bit on it. As if seizing an opportunity that would blossom by unburdening himself, he began to methodically disclose the details of the operations he had carried out at the behest of his MIS handler. One in particular was especially unsettling.

Omar confided that he had managed to get perilously close to the local CIA operation's two communications, or "commo," officers. To appreciate the magnitude of that, think of these commo officers as the predecessors of present-day systems administrators. Systems administrator is the position that was held by Edward Snowden, the National Security Agency contractor who publicly disclosed details of the NSA's highly classified counterterrorism operations, beginning in the spring of 2013. Just as in the case of systems administrators, the nature of the commo officers' job gives them full access to all of the information stored at, and transmitted to and from, their location.

The two commo officers shared a house in the city, and Omar had scored a huge win: He had recruited the servant who worked in the house. Having eyes and ears embedded in the home of the commo officers had Omar's MIS handler salivating at the prospects. Fortunately for U.S. interests, the threat disappeared within a month. Omar said the servant got a better offer to work at the home of an employee with one of the other foreign missions in the city—one in which the MIS had absolutely no interest. When Omar gave the news to his handler, a hulking man who had been a competitive weightlifter, the Menacian was livid. He lashed out at Omar, who didn't grasp the enormity of the situation.

"You fool!" the Menacian seethed, shaking with rage. "Those two had gold in their heads!"

Omar's revelations continued through the night. As dawn approached, the casual nature of the conversation was almost surreal. Omar was chatting with Phil as if he was talking about what he did on his summer vacation. He was focusing on what Phil needed him to focus on—he was in short-term thinking mode. Phil had gotten him to that place.

When it was all over, Phil gazed out of the window that Omar had approached with the towel those many hours earlier. It seemed like an eternity ago. The rush of what had

## INTERROGATION/ELICITATION

A process that is designed to influence or persuade an individual to reveal information that he has reason to want to conceal.

transpired since then hadn't ebbed, so he didn't feel tired. But he was definitely ready to make up for that dinner he missed.

# 3.

# TRANSITIONING TO INTERROGATION MODE: THE DOC AND THE DOG

||||||||||||||||||||||||||||||||||||||||||||||||||

Consider the perfect burglary. It occurs when a burglar enters the target building without being detected, conducts the theft, and leaves—with no one the wiser.

If we think of Omar's case as a burglary, he was well on his way to committing the perfect crime. He escaped detection when he entered. He conducted his pilferage for years without being discovered. But when he sat down with Phil in that hotel suite, he hadn't succeeded in his mission, because he had yet to make an undetected getaway.

The two were engaged in a complex mental showdown. Omar was evaluating Phil, just as Phil was evaluating Omar. Phil had been in that position plenty of times before, and he was well aware of the weapons his opponent possessed to use against him. Looming largest was Omar's willingness and determination to deceive. There was, in addition, Omar's ability at some level to disguise that deception. And then there was, no doubt, some degree of confidence that he would be able to accomplish his aim.

Phil's plan of attack began with an assault on Omar's

confidence. That entailed sending him a very clear message: *Your mission has failed. Everything you have done up to this point to accomplish your mission—the hidden path to success that you thought you were on—has ended in failure, because you didn't get out. You were caught on the inside, committing the act. You have no choice now but to change your strategy.*

Phil and Omar were each in a position to help the other. Phil needed information and cooperation from Omar; Omar needed a new game plan, because his old one failed. Phil's task was to offer him a replacement strategy in a way that didn't cause Omar to throw up his defenses, and that didn't alert him to the fact that at that moment, Phil was switching from interview mode to interrogation mode. What marked the switch—and what initiated the message—is what we call the *transition statement*.

The transition statement is the first sentence or two of the monologue. It takes the form of a *direct observation of concern* (DOC), a *direct observation of guilt* (DOG), or some variant that falls between the two.

The DOC lies at one end of what you might think of as your own confidence spectrum. Imagine you're the manager at a pharmacy, and the pharmacist has informed you that several dozen oxycodone tablets are missing. You're interviewing one of the pharmacy technicians—we'll call her "Jan"—about the missing tablets, and she appears to be having a problem. Some of the behaviors she exhibits—perhaps some inconsistencies in her story, perhaps instances of evasiveness—lead you to determine that it's time to go into interrogation mode. At this point you have your suspicions about Jan, but you realize there's a lot you still don't know. You decide to convey a DOC, which might go something like this:

"Jan, I want you to know that your cooperation is very helpful, and I really do appreciate it. The thing is, some of what you're saying just isn't adding up, and I need you to help me understand what I'm missing."

Now, let's say that after speaking with the pharmacist and reviewing the dispensing records and time sheets, it's clear that despite her denials, the only person who could have taken the oxycodone is Jan. Your confidence level is over on the high end of the spectrum, so your transition statement becomes a DOG:

"Jan, I have to tell you, based on our conversation, based on the inquiry we've conducted, based on all the facts we've collected, there's no doubt that you're the person who took the oxycodone."

As we mentioned, your transition statement might be a variant that falls somewhere in between the two, depending on your level of confidence. Let's say all indications are that Jan is the one who took the oxycodone, but you have just enough doubt to be compelled to leave the door open to the possibility that she didn't do it. In that case, your transition statement might be something along these lines:

"Jan, at this point we know the *what*. We also know the *who*. But what we don't know is the *why*. And that's what you and I need to talk about."

Jan got the message—she's pretty much busted. But you've delivered it without being as direct, and with just enough wiggle room to back out if you need to. Bear in mind that in all three cases, even though the language changes, the statements are delivered in precisely the same manner—your tone is low-key, your voice is soft, and your pace is unrushed. By the very nature of the circumstances, you're in an adversarial position. But you're pulling the rug out from under that fact with your delivery.

Note, as well, that the words you use to convey your message need to be well chosen. In the DOG, you referred to an "inquiry," not an investigation. You said she "took" the oxycodone, she didn't "steal" it. Those nuances help to keep Jan in short-term thinking mode. It's important to use language that doesn't trigger consequential thoughts—like the prospect of getting fired, or serving jail time.

The beauty of the transition statement is that it immediately conveys to the individual that nothing she has done up to that point to try to beat you has worked, yet that painful message is delivered below the radar, where it doesn't trigger her defenses and create an adversarial relationship. Now she's thinking, since what she's been doing has been unsuccessful, where does she go from here? How should she handle it? Should she give you a little bit? Should she try to blame it on someone else? She's trying to rethink her game plan, and guess what. You're right there to give her some other things to think about. Since everything she was thinking about before just blew up in her face, what you give her to think about might just sound pretty good—especially when it's delivered in such a low-key, nonconfrontational manner.

That's why a shift into interrogation mode that involves launching into a fist-pounding, vein-popping rant as a means of getting a person to tell you something he wants to conceal is so fundamentally counterproductive. You've given him something else to think about, all right. You've motivated him to draw the battle lines, identify you as the enemy, and entrench himself in resistance. Your job has just become exponentially more difficult.

Beyond that, a person who's being deceptive is incentivized to do everything in his power to try to get the spotlight off of himself, and onto someone else. Since you're a natural, and very convenient, target of the attempted shift, you need to recognize that if you start getting aggressive and verbally abusive, the deceptive person is likely to try to twist that to his advantage. Suddenly, he's interviewing you about why you're mistreating him, and you're getting nowhere. If you remain unruffled and soft-spoken, you take that option off the table, and you remain in control.

Now, let's go back and look at Phil's encounter with Omar. When Phil asked that fateful question about whether Omar had ever worked for another intelligence service, the reality was that it was an extremely broad question. So when Omar responded with what Phil identified as deceptive behavior, now it was Phil who was being presented with a question to be answered: What part of that broad question was troubling Omar?

When confronted with the task of narrowing down the possibilities, there's a tendency to start to think about what the problem might be. Often, the natural inclination is to ask more questions to try to pinpoint where the issue lies on the best-case/worst-case continuum. But there's an inherent danger in that, as Phil had learned the hard way when he interviewed Mary: Trying to do any pinpointing before the shift into interrogation mode can backfire, big-time. During the interview, we determine from the person's behavior what it is he wants to hide, and we begin to narrow down the likely parameters we're dealing with along the continuum. It's only in the course of the interrogation that we're able to determine where, within those parameters, the situation falls.

When he decided the pivotal moment had come to shift into interrogation mode, Phil delivered a transition statement in the form of a DOC that kept the parameters wide open: "Omar, there's clearly something here that you're not telling me, that we need to talk about." At that moment, Phil had no idea whether the issue he was dealing with was something on the order of Omar's son hanging out with some unsavory characters who may have had a connection to another intelligence service, or Omar working as an operative against U.S. interests at the behest of the MIS. But he did know that his DOC covered both possibilities. No doubt, because of what he understood to be Omar's unblemished record, Phil's head was at the best-case end of the continuum. But the methodology saved him by ensuring that his interrogation covered the full range of possibilities across the spectrum.

The methodology also has a valuable confirmatory element to it. When Phil said there was "something" Omar wasn't telling him, that unspecified "something" likely caused Omar to selectively orient himself to what the real problem was. So when it was time for Omar to talk, there was a high probability that Phil would be able to identify the issue, or to at least collect enough clues to enable him to confirm its location on the spectrum.

One more thing: It's essential to remember that Omar's reaction might not have equaled the face value of the question. That is, if Omar had been clean rather than dirty, for example, any deceptive behavior he exhibited in response to Phil's question about working for another intelligence service would have been something that was relatively inconsequential, like that he had failed to mention being approached by someone he suspected of working for the bad guys. By interrogating to the full length of the spectrum, Phil would likely be successful in getting Omar to admit that failure. If he discovered that was the extent of the problem, Phil would probably say something like this:

"Omar, thanks. I'm glad you told me. We're not really concerned about that, so I'm glad we were able to resolve it."

In clean Omar's mind, even though he messed up, he was treated fairly and respectfully, and his loyalty and dedication to U.S. interests are bolstered. The relationship with this key asset remains solid. No damage was done. We'll elaborate on the value of that in Chapter 10.

The transition statement is an exhilarating point in the interrogation, with a rush second only to the moment when you actually get the truth. Formulating the transition statement is exciting, because it's the first time you communicate to the person that you know he did the bad thing, whether you convey that implicitly or explicitly. It's the strength of the person's reaction to your statement that's so telling, because it often signals the level of resistance you'll likely encounter the rest of the way. From a behavior analysis standpoint, the reaction to the transition statement can reinforce your confidence in whether the person is being deceptive. For example, if, in response to the transition statement, "Our investigation indicates that you're involved in some way," the person sits in silence, or responds with something like, "I can't think of anything that would bother me about an investigation," you know you're on the right course. By failing to state with conviction that there's nothing about an investigation that would bother him, he's sending you the unintended message that there's something there, but you haven't given him a reason to share it with you. What he doesn't realize is you're about to give it to him with your monologue.

At first blush, the DOC and the DOG may appear to be rather mechanical and easy to master. That's not the case at all. While the transition statement is somewhat formulaic in the sense that it's a prepared statement that appears at the beginning of the monologue, there is actually a rather complex set of strategic psychological considerations that arise in selecting the phraseology. How well crafted your transition statement is sets the tone of the interrogation to follow and, more often than not, determines whether you'll be successful.

The accusatory strength of the DOC and DOG depends upon a number of factors. Let's say, for example, that your

## TRANSITION STATEMENTS

Here's a list of some sample transition statements that illustrate the gradation from gentle to strong along the scale from direct observation of concern to direct observation of guilt:

- You seem to be thinking about something.
- Something is clearly on your mind.
- Something seems to be bothering you when we talk about . . .
- You seem uncertain when you say . . .
- When I ask you about _____, I can see some concern on your face.
- I'm a little uncomfortable with your answer.
- I have some concerns about what you're telling me.
- Based on our conversation, it appears you have more to tell us.
- I think you need to rethink your answer.
- I have a problem with some of the things you've told me.
- We've completed our investigation and, frankly, we can't eliminate you from our list of suspects.
- Our investigation indicates that you are involved in some way.
- Our investigation clearly shows that you . . .
- I'm absolutely certain that I know the *who* and the *what*. Now all I need to understand is the *why*.

transition statement is, "Our investigation clearly shows that you're the one who took the money." That statement lies on the extreme end of the DOG side of the scale, and it can backfire on you because it sets the person up to make a denial. That's something you want to listen for during the interview, but you want to avoid in an interrogation situation. You already have one hurdle to overcome: getting the person to tell the truth. If you allow him to voice a denial, you have a second, equally formidable hurdle: getting the person to admit that he's a liar. That scenario can easily degenerate into endless head-butting and frustration, and getting the truth becomes far more difficult.

That's not to say that the DOG, "Our investigation clearly shows that you did it," is never appropriate—it can be the most appropriate transition statement to use. The point is to ensure that your approach in determining the strength of your transition statement is governed by careful consideration of a range of factors, including your level of confidence, the sensitivity of the issue under investigation, the political dynamics, and the person's level of sophistication. The transition statement is highly nuanced, so it's best to have a number of arrows in your transition statement quiver that you can pull out, depending on the circumstances of the interrogation situation.

# 4.

# UNCOVERING A SPY: THE ART OF CREATING THE MONOLOGUE

||||||||||||||||||||||||||||||||||||

(*Authors' note: Due to the sensitive nature of the case we're discussing in this chapter, the foreign country involved can't be disclosed. We'll refer to it by the fictitious name, Foeland, and to its citizens as* Foelandians.)

At the World Cup soccer games held in a picturesque city outside of the United States in the not-too-distant past, a stocky, bespectacled young man we'll call "Lee" was hard at work. Not a Foelandian (nor indeed a U.S. citizen) but a specialist in Foelandian studies who was fluent in the language, Lee had been appointed as an interpreter for the Foelandian team. It was a demanding assignment, requiring round-the-clock availability for the duration of the event. That was fine with Lee—he valued the opportunity to put his skills to use in such a prestigious setting, and the simple truth was he enjoyed being around Foelandians. The time he spent with the soccer players and their Foelandian overseers was a valuable immersion opportunity that, for Lee, rivaled a visit to Foeland.

Not surprisingly, several of the Foelandian overseers were agents of the Foelandian Intelligence Service, or FIS. One of those agents, whom we'll call "Otto," had struck up an especially friendly relationship with Lee, and the two often talked about their families and what they hoped to do with their lives. One evening, as they were leaving the dorm that housed the team, Otto asked Lee about his plans for pursuing his Foelandian studies. Lee said his dream was to get a graduate degree, and he was torn between universities in the United States and in Foeland.

Lee eventually decided that since it was often difficult for foreigners to study in Foeland, he would opt for the United States. Before long, he was enrolled in a graduate program at a prestigious university that had a highly regarded Foelandian studies program. Shortly after he arrived, he met a fellow student, an American we'll call "Nate," and they quickly became good friends. When they finished their studies, they went their separate ways to pursue their careers. Lee returned to his home country, and was hired as a researcher and specialist in Foelandian studies. Nate went on to serve as a case officer with the CIA.

As the years passed, Nate and Lee stayed in touch, at least to the extent of sending the occasional greeting card. And then, just by chance, Nate was transferred to Lee's home country. He reestablished contact with his friend, and soon learned that Lee's research position gave him access to information that was of high interest to the U.S. government. Nate recognized the potential intelligence value of that connection, but he certainly didn't want to do anything to jeopardize his friendship with Lee. He ultimately decided to approach Lee with the idea of becoming an asset for the Agency. When Lee proved to be open to the idea, Nate was both gratified by the potential intelligence coup, and relieved that his friendship with Lee was unharmed.

When the time came to bring Lee on board, the process of vetting him began. Phil was soon on a flight to Lee's home country—it would be up to him to ensure that Lee was clean.

The plan was for Nate to arrange for Lee to arrive at a designated suite at a hotel in the country's capital at six that evening. Phil and Nate got there early enough to ensure that they had plenty of time to check out the suite. They agreed it would be best for Nate to excuse himself after Lee arrived. Unfortunately for Nate, the only place available for him to wait it out was the bathroom.

"You can wait down in the lobby if you want," Phil said. He was unsurprised when Nate declined. Nate was a good case officer, and Lee was his guy. There was no way he was leaving—he wanted at least to be able to hear what was going on. Phil stressed to Nate that he had to be as quiet as possible, because if Lee could hear him, he'd know the reverse was also the case. If there was something Phil needed to elicit that Lee wanted to conceal, knowing his friend could hear would cause Lee to become that much more deeply entrenched in his concealment. If Nate had to flush the toilet, Phil instructed, fine. Other than that, silence. It was a fundamental tenet of the profession: Nobody confesses to a crowd.

Lee showed up right on time at six o'clock. Nate introduced him to Phil, and with this-is-how-we-do-it-all-the-time nonchalance, retired to the bathroom.

Phil and Lee took their seats. As Phil began the interview, he could see that Lee seemed nervous. While he took note of that fact, he knew that some degree of nervousness was natural under the circumstances, so he had no inclination to jump to any conclusions about what was causing it. Lee wasn't exhibiting any deceptive behavior in response to Phil's questions, and that's what mattered. It was all going quite well, in fact, when Phil got to the question about whether Lee had ever worked for the bad guys.

"Lee, this next question is very important," Phil said

gently. "You're willing to work for us—have you ever worked for any other foreign intelligence organization?"

Phil thought he'd seen it all. He hadn't. Lee paused. Then he stood up, said, "No, sir," and sat back down. He lowered his head and stared at the floor.

*Are you kidding me?* Phil's mind was reeling. It was as if this scholarly researcher had suddenly turned the clock back to the formal academic environment of his youth, and had been chastised by the headmaster. *What was that all about?*

The answer, as always, lay somewhere on the best-case/worst-case continuum. In any event, it was weird. Lee and Nate were longtime friends, and now Phil had to determine what was up with Lee's disturbing reaction to the "are you working for the bad guys" question. There was no doubt that Lee was troubled by the question, so it was time for Phil's ideational fluency to kick in. He had a monologue to deliver, and he did so, calmly and reassuringly, beginning with a transition statement that took the form of a DOC.

"Lee, I know this isn't an easy interview, by any means, and that some of the questions are very personal," Phil said. "There's clearly something that's bothering you, and we need to talk about that."

Lee was leaning forward slightly, with his head down. It appeared he had something to say, but he was silent. Phil continued, his pace unrushed, no edginess in his voice, no recrimination in his tone.

"Lee, this situation is somewhat awkward, I know. After all, you and Nate are really good friends, and have been for a long time. In fact, Nate was telling me about some of the things you guys have done together over the years, and it was obvious how much he values your friendship. He thinks the world of you, Lee, and he has the utmost respect for your background, and the knowledge you have, and the way you're using that knowledge for the greater good. That's why he approached you about working with us in the first place, Lee—he knows you can do so much good for so many people, given the opportunity."

Lee looked up at Phil, and looked back down. Again, he said nothing. Phil was on a roll.

"We were talking earlier, and the only concern he expressed was that you might not realize how things work in our world, and what we encounter all the time. He was worried that you might think that something could disqualify you, when in reality there's not a whole lot we haven't seen and been able to work through. You know, Nate was saying you're kind of a perfectionist, and the fact is, we live in an imperfect world, Lee."

In the bathroom, Nate was struggling to hear Phil's lowered voice. What he was hearing was making him crazy. *He's not even twenty minutes into it, and he's interrogating my guy? What the hell is he doing?* Phil was just getting started.

"We talk with guys all the time who think they have to be perfect. That's not the way it works, Lee. It just isn't. Listen, this is a little bit awkward for me, too, you know? Nate's my friend, too, and of course I don't want to have to deliver any bad news to him. But that's just it, Lee—it doesn't have to be bad news. There's no reason in the world why it has to be bad news. Because whatever it is that's bothering you, you have to understand it can be fixed. It's a fixable problem. It's nothing we haven't dealt with before, nothing that would surprise us. I've been doing this for a long time, Lee, and I can tell you, there's not a single problem that's ever come up in this kind of a situation that we haven't been able to work through and fix. Because we know that people do things for all kinds of reasons, and sometimes those reasons just involve things that lie outside their control. Sometimes they just don't realize how serious something might be, or that it's a problem at all. They simply haven't thought their way through the whole thing."

By this time, Phil was starting to get repetitive. Of course, that was the whole idea. Remember the infomercial analogy? The more frequently a person hears something, the more likely he is to accept it, or to at least be open to the possibility of accepting it. Phil kept going for the better part of an hour. Lee sat the entire time with his head down, not saying a word. Finally, Phil decided it was time to test the water. He needed to know where Lee's head was at. To do that, he had to give Lee a chance to talk. Phil paused, and with the compassionate voice of a caring mentor, he took that next step.

"Lee, when I asked you about working for another intelligence service, who were you thinking about?"

After a momentary pause, Lee looked up, seemingly mustering the courage to formulate the words. "The Foelandians," he said.

There it was. Okay. Phil nodded with a look of finally understanding what Lee was going through.

"Thank you, Lee. That makes perfect sense. Let's face it, your life's work has been built around associating with and understanding the Foelandian people. And you know what? I don't blame you a bit. I've always been fascinated by Foeland, too, and I've often thought about how incredible it would be to travel through the country, and to meet the people and see everything. But I don't have that option, because it's just too hard, Lee. Because of the way things are in the world, there are just too many hoops to jump through."

Lee looked up. Phil seemed to be striking a chord.

"So regardless of all the political stuff, Lee, I can fully understand why you would be attracted to the Foelandian people. I just need to have an understanding of why you were thinking about the Foelandians when I asked you the question about working for another intelligence service, Lee. So let's talk about it. Let's at least do that."

Lee nodded. "Okay," he said.

After taking a moment to collect his thoughts, he began his story by taking Phil back to the World Cup, when he met Otto. He said Otto had introduced him to a Foelandian friend of his who lived in the city where the university he was attending was located. Lee said he and this friend of Otto's, whom we'll call "Horace," also struck up a friendship, and that they often talked about Lee's studies and his acquaintances in the university. He said he had applied for a position as a research assistant to one of the senior faculty members, and when he mentioned to Horace that he had been accepted, the Foelandian seemed to be especially interested in the connection. Lee said this particular faculty member served as an advisor to U.S. policymakers, and that fact appeared to be what had piqued Horace's interest. Horace would often ask about the advisory work the faculty member was performing for the government, Lee said, acknowledging that he would occasionally provide Horace with copies of documents pertaining to the faculty member's government-related activities.

By that point, Phil fully recognized that the issue he was dealing with was perilously close to the worst-case edge of the continuum. He went back into his monologue. This time, the transition was from DOC to DOG.

"Lee, thank you for sharing that with me, it's tremendously helpful. It's become very clear that what we're dealing with here is your work with Horace in an intelligence-gathering capacity, and having that out in the open makes this so much easier to fix. Lee, please understand that in our world, this is the sort of thing we see all the time. I've worked with people from all walks of life—mothers, fathers, students, government officials, corporate executives—who have found themselves in exactly the same situation we're looking at right now. The reason is that genuinely good people sometimes get in over their heads, and before they know it, they're thinking, 'Jeez, how did I get into this?' They got into it because their hearts were in the right place. I mean, let's face it: Your Foelandian friends have helped and supported you over the years, and it's only natural to want to repay them somehow. If someone does you a favor, it's just natural to want to do him a favor in return. That's just natural, Lee. I understand that, Nate understands that, everybody understands that. Maybe your Foelandian friends took advantage of you— I don't know, that's not my call, and I'm not going to sit here in judgment of anybody. What I do know is that this is a fixable problem. But in order to fix it, we need to get everything out on the table so we know what we're dealing with. That's the only way. So, Lee, who do you think these people were that you were gathering this information for?"

Lee shrugged.

"Come on, Lee," Phil said, his voice as calm and measured as it had been all along. "You know who they were, right?"

Lee nodded.

"Who were they, Lee?" Phil asked.

Lee looked at Phil. "Same as you," he said.

"No, Lee. No. Who were they?" Phil's tone was gently encouraging, as if he was eager to help Lee lift an enormous weight off his chest.

Lee's head dropped. "FIS," he said, referring to the Foelandian Intelligence Service.

In the bathroom, Nate closed his eyes, and shook his head. This longtime friend was an FIS asset. It seemed unthinkable, and yet he had heard it himself, straight from Lee. His mind started to drift off to some of the times he had spent with his friend, but he snapped it back. He needed to hear the rest, but at that point Phil decided to give Lee a breather.

"Thank you for that," Phil said. "I know that wasn't easy. Tell you what. Let's take a break."

Phil went into the bathroom. There was Nate, still shaking his head.

"I was going to *kill* you," Nate said. Phil wasn't sure whether Nate was most perturbed about the interview having transitioned to an interrogation, Lee's revelation, or just being stuck in the tiny bathroom for the duration of what seemed like an interminable monologue.

"Yeah, I'm sorry, Nate," Phil said, knowing this had to be tough on him.

"No, you played it exactly right," Nate conceded. "We have to get to the bottom of this." He apparently felt better after venting.

"I will," Phil assured him. "Just be patient." Nate nodded. They agreed they would go for as long as it took.

Phil sat back down with Lee, and continued where he had left off. The rest was painful, but it could have been worse. Lee admitted that when he and Nate were at the university, he had informed his FIS handlers that Nate might be applying to work at the CIA or the FBI. He said they encouraged him to maintain and deepen the friendship.

Lee said when he graduated and returned to his home country, he was introduced to a new Foelandian contact, and he acknowledged to Phil that he knew the contact was a FIS agent. Phil asked what had persuaded him to work with the FIS, and whether it was for financial gain. Lee responded that he had occasionally received small sums of cash, but that wasn't what enticed him.

"Then why are you doing this?" Phil asked.

Lee seemed almost embarrassed by the simplicity of it all. "I like Foelandians," he said.

Back in the bathroom, Nate was listening intently. *Ask him, Phil.*

It was as if Phil could read Nate's mind. He asked Lee if he had told his FIS handlers that Nate had recruited him to work for the Agency. Lee said he had not, and confessed that what he was most ashamed of was telling them about Nate when they were back at the university. Lee showed no signs of deceptive behavior in his response. He had simply been torn in two directions: He just liked Foelandians, and he liked his good friend, Nate, too.

At eight o'clock the next morning, fourteen hours after it had begun, Phil's work was done. Nate, on the other hand, had more work to do. He was livid that Lee had betrayed him, but the pain of that betrayal was mitigated by the fact that Lee hadn't reported his recent contacts with Nate, or his recruitment. A couple of weeks later, Nate, along with an FBI agent, took Lee back to the city where the university was located, and they went to all the places where Lee had met with his FIS handlers. Among the information passed to the FBI were the identities of those handlers.

With the Lee case at the top of our mind, then, our next step is to dive a little more deeply into the delivery and the content of the all-important monologue. We'll begin that dive in the next chapter.

# 5.
# HOW TO DELIVER YOUR MONOLOGUE
||||||||||||||||||||||||||||||||||||||||

We've heard it said that a guilty person just wants to be understood, because being understood allows him to feel that he's been forgiven. That observation encapsulates what the monologue is designed and executed to accomplish. When Phil was interrogating Lee, he never lost sight of the fact that he had neither the power to forgive him for whatever it was he was concealing, nor the authority to decide that there would be no serious consequences for his actions. But Phil knew that if Lee could, on some level, be convinced that his questioner could grasp the situation from his perspective, the chances of getting the truth out of him would rise tremendously. So how do we go about giving the person we're interrogating the impression that we *understand* him?

It isn't easy. It certainly wasn't easy for Phil when he was interrogating Mary. After all, he detested that woman for what she had done: She had betrayed her country—*his* country. And yet, when it was all over, Mary felt moved to hug Phil, and as she hugged him, to say, "Thank you for understanding." Of course, nothing could have been further from the truth of the matter. It was far beyond Phil's comprehension how anyone could have engaged in such a betrayal. He couldn't even begin to understand it. But in Mary's mind, he understood.

Nor was it easy for Michael Floyd, when he was called in some years ago to assist in the investigation of a young father who had been accused of inflicting serious injuries on his three-month-old baby boy. Those injuries included several broken ribs, bruises that covered the baby's back, and a seriously swollen liver. Thanks in large part to the rapport Michael was able to establish with the father in the course of the interrogation, the father confessed. For that to happen, Michael had to be perceived as being truly understanding, and as genuinely sincere.

A lot of people try to take what we do and apply it, but they're unsuccessful because the missing element is sincerity. That person sitting in front of you has to believe that you mean what you're saying. So you have to either genuinely be sincere, or have the ability to create an appearance of sincerity that's equal to, or at least close to, genuine. In many instances, like Michael's interrogation of this father, that will require a stellar acting job.

There's an acting device we've found to be very helpful in selling that perception of sincerity—we refer to it by the acronym SEL. Here's what it entails:

## Slow your rate of speech

Keep in mind that when you transition to the monologue, your adrenaline will likely be kicking in. There's a lot at stake, and you're going for it—this is the big play. Make a conscious effort to speak slowly and distinctly. Placing an emphasis on some of the key words will help you slow down. The idea is to come across as unrushed and controlled, which in turn creates a more easygoing, relaxed mood.

## Engage the person you're interrogating

There's no reason to take notes—the person isn't saying anything, remember? So put your pen and notebook down. Absorb yourself in the person-to-person contact, without staring at him, or locking eyes with him. It may not be a cozy fireside chat, but the discomfort of the situation can be minimized with this engagement.

## Lower your voice

Our experience has corroborated a great deal of research that has shown that as a control mechanism, a lower volume is much more effective than a higher volume. If you start yelling at someone, typically the natural reaction is twofold: First, he'll probably yell back. Second, he'll almost certainly tune you out, and that's the worst thing that can happen. The first mistake he made was to allow you to talk. He doesn't realize that you've stopped asking questions, and now you're the one who's doing the talking. The longer that goes on, the more it works to your advantage. To keep it going, it's essential to stay low-key, and a voice that's lowered a decibel or two aids that effort tremendously.

Keep in mind that as critical as the *content* of the monologue is, *delivery* trumps it—it's that important. No matter how brilliant and compelling what you're saying is, if it isn't delivered effectively, the person you're interrogating won't even hear it. If your manner is harsh and overbearing, he'll see you as an opponent, and he'll be thinking of nothing but ways to fight you. You might as well be speaking a foreign language, because he's translating whatever you're saying as, "I'm out to get you." The moment that happens, your job just got exponentially more difficult.

With your voice as your instrument of influence, your aim is to build and maintain whatever level of rapport you can in that situation. He may not like you, or like the position you represent. But all of a sudden, the way you're talking to him, he's likely thinking, "Wow, this isn't what I was expecting at all. I expected to get brow-beaten." You may still get some resistance, but if he sees you as someone who's treating him respectfully and professionally, someone who's objective rather than out to get him, someone who doesn't appear to be an enemy, his resistance will be dampened significantly. The beautiful part is it's all working to your advantage rather than to his, but he doesn't know that.

When Phil began his monologue in his interrogation of Lee, the first two sentences after the DOC were these:

"Lee, this situation is somewhat awkward, I know. After all, you and Nate are really good friends, and have been for a long time."

With that sympathetic sentiment, Phil was conveying to Lee that he got it. He could understand what Lee must be feeling, and he cared. There was certainly nothing extemporaneous about that sentiment, nor about the timing of it. It couldn't have been more deliberate. An excellent rule of thumb is to make sure that the sentence immediately following the transition statement is a statement of sympathy or empathy. That way, the person hears right up front exactly what you want him to hear. Phil's expression of sympathy primed the pump for Lee to receive the monologue in the right frame of mind.

At the point when Lee admitted that what he had been thinking about was "the Foelandians," Phil jumped on the opportunity to convey an empathetic sentiment:

"I've always been fascinated by Foeland, too, and I've often thought about how incredible it would be to travel through the country, and to meet the people and see everything."

Now, Phil not only sympathizes with Lee, he empathizes with him—he not only cares, but he has felt what Lee was feeling. We need to make it clear that this particular expression of empathy raises a point that warrants discussion: Phil's statement wasn't true. He's never had any desire whatsoever to visit Foeland. The takeaway here is that what you say in your monologue needs to be relevant and believable, but not necessarily factual (we'll explore this topic further in Chapter 9). Certainly, the truth stretching can never go so far as to promise something you can't deliver as a means of eliciting a confession. But coming across as sincere is absolutely essential, and accomplishing that sometimes forces you to lie, especially when feeling any sense of genuine sympathy is simply impossible. Try to imagine, for example, that you had to interrogate a serial child molester. Phil doesn't have to try to imagine it. He experienced it.

Early in his career, Phil had been called in to interview a U.S. government employee who held a senior managerial position. The man, whom we'll call "Oscar," was under investigation for child molestation. Phil had routinely been called upon to conduct interviews and interrogations of people who were accused of committing some of the most horrific crimes imaginable. It was part of the job, and it had to be done. But this one was especially tough.

The ongoing investigation of Oscar had not yielded any conclusive evidence against him. The problem was that Oscar had failed several polygraph examinations, because he was having trouble with standard questions about sexual deviancy. That process had isolated deception with respect to sexual activity involving children, and Oscar never budged from his adamant insistence that he had never engaged in any such activity.

Oscar knew very well why he had been instructed by the security department to meet with Phil, so there was no need for pretense. Phil reviewed the polygraph results with Oscar. Unruffled, and with characteristic calm, Phil asked the question that had to be asked: Had Oscar ever engaged in sexual activity involving children?

Oscar scowled. He wagged his finger at Phil, and with unmasked contempt, responded.

"Young man, I would never do that," Oscar bristled, glaring at Phil. "That would be perverted, and I am not a pervert."

Phil didn't need to hear any more from Oscar. It was time for Oscar to do the listening, so Phil transitioned into interrogation mode.

"Oscar, it's obvious from the consistent results we're getting from our polygraph exams that there's something you're thinking about that involves sexual activity with children, and we need to talk about that so we can clear it up. Listen, I happen to have two little boys of my own. Quite frankly, if I thought you were a pervert, I don't think I could stay in the same room with you. I couldn't do it. But that's not what this is about. This is about finding out what's bothering somebody who's been serving his country with distinction for a long time. Whatever it is that's bothering you, Oscar, I guarantee you, it's not the end of the world. If it were, we might as well all kiss the world good-bye, because we've all done things that we wish we hadn't done, and that bother us when we think about them. Those things happen, Oscar, without anyone wanting to cause any harm. In these situations, what we often find is that stuff happens, and it happens to good people. What I mean by that is we have situations where bad people do bad things. But sometimes good people simply make the wrong decisions. They don't intend to hurt anyone, they just end up going too far sometimes, not realizing what the consequences are, or that anyone is really being harmed. If that's the case here, Oscar, we need to talk about it so we can fix it. You know, I'm not a psychiatrist, and I don't pretend to be. But I do know that sometimes things happen in our lives, often when we're young, that cause us to do things later in life that we have absolutely no control over. If we did, they would never have happened. I also know that we live in a crazy world, Oscar. I mean, everywhere you look, you're bombarded with sex, and you can't get away from it. That's a social problem, and one that society has to fix. We can't fix that, Oscar. But we *can* fix this, as long as we address it openly and honestly."

It was going well. What Phil was saying was apparently resonating, because Oscar wasn't putting up any resistance. Phil kept going, repeating the points he was making, and repeating them again. When the time came to test the water, Phil did so gently, and with no hint of derision or sanctimony.

"Oscar, I know all of this is very embarrassing to have to talk about. Nobody wants to be in a position of talking about things that are very, very personal. Talking about things involving children is especially embarrassing in the society we live in, there's no question about that. But sometimes the situation involves children, and let's face it, kids are everywhere. Now, when was the last time you were alone with any of these kids?"

The disturbing nature of the rest of the conversation was such that we certainly have no intention of subjecting anyone to it here. What we can say is that Oscar admitted to molesting hundreds of children. He even shared his favorite hangout when he was on the prowl: a popular pizza and arcade chain that catered to children.

Now, let's go back to the beginning of Phil's monologue,

and look at what he said when he was addressing Oscar's seething claim that he wasn't a pervert:

"Listen, I happen to have two little boys of my own. Quite frankly, if I thought you were a pervert, I don't think I could stay in the same room with you."

That statement wasn't entirely untrue. Phil did, in fact, have two little boys at the time. But the indication that he didn't think Oscar was a pervert, and that he wouldn't be able to sit in the same room with him if that were the case, was untrue. Phil thought Oscar was as perverted as they come, and being in the same room with him made his skin crawl. Still, he knew he had to neutralize Oscar's attempt to convince him that he wasn't a pervert so that Oscar would abandon that tack. The best way to do that was to agree with him, notwithstanding the untruthfulness of the statement. The moment Phil said that, Oscar lost a key play in his game plan, and he was put in the position of having to rethink his approach. And Phil was right there to help him figure it out.

We're occasionally asked a question about all of this that may have occurred to you, as well: Why don't truly evil, coldhearted, hardened people, like Oscar, or perhaps a terrorist who senselessly kills innocent people, see this noncoercive approach as an indication of weakness or impotence that, far from compelling them to cooperate, encourages them toward what they perceive as an easy conquest?

Our response is to consider the underlying premise of the question. What, exactly, does it mean to be evil, coldhearted, and hardened? And to what extent is our own perception of those conditions authentic? To contend that those conditions equate to "I'm not going to cooperate or talk" is to impose our own logic—indeed, our own bias—on the behavior of another person. The truth is, human behavior isn't necessarily logical, nor can it be expected to conform to our own expectations or biases. After all, what's logical about molesting children? A psychologist at the Agency put it this way: There's only a casual relationship between human behavior and logic. We simply cannot allow ourselves to assume that bad guys, or anyone else for that matter, will behave in a particular way under a particular circumstance. Our experience has borne that out, over and over again.

Susan Carnicero once conducted a screening interview with a job candidate we'll call "Lucille," who had acknowledged in a preliminary interview with one of Susan's associates that she had had some drug problems in the past, but she stressed that she had long ago overcome them. When Susan met with her for the interview, Lucille arrived very casually dressed in a blue work shirt and blue jeans. The shirt had a logo on it, and as Susan proceeded with the interview, she found herself looking at the logo and trying to figure out what it was. It turned out to be the logo of the prison where Lucille had just finished serving time for possession of cocaine with intent to distribute. She had to leave directly from the interview with Susan to check into a halfway house, where she was being assigned to help her continue her fight against drug addiction. The relationship between Lucille's behavior and logic was even more casual than her interview attire.

# 6.

# HOW TO TAILOR YOUR MONOLOGUE

||||||||||||||||||||||||||||||||||||||||

At first glance, it might have appeared that Phil's monologue in his interrogation of Lee was just a random stream of consciousness, a free-form flow of encouraging comments that spilled out in the hope that some part of it would coax Lee to fess up. That's not the case at all. While the aim was indeed to persuade Lee to divulge everything he was attempting to conceal, not a word Phil said in the monologue was extraneous to that deliberate intent. Every sentence in his narrative had a distinct, thoughtful objective; each one was consciously woven into a meaningful whole, with no scraps left over to diminish its effectiveness.

Let's take a look at the components we use to build a monologue, why we use them, and how they were used in Phil's interrogation of Lee. Note that there's no particular order in which the components should necessarily appear in the monologue.

## Rationalizing the action

There is not a single thing a person can do that cannot be rationalized. You can come up with a reason, or an excuse, for absolutely anything. In a monologue, it's a face-saving exercise that's extremely effective in the quest to keep the person in short-term thinking mode. Here are a couple of examples of how Phil used rationalization in Lee's case:

- "The reason is that genuinely good people sometimes get in over their heads, and before they know it, they're thinking, 'Jeez, how did I get into this?' They got into it because their hearts were in the right place. I mean, let's face it: Your Foelandian friends have helped and supported you over the years, and it's only natural to want to repay them somehow. If someone does you a favor, it's just natural to want to do him a favor in return."
- "Because we know that people do things for all kinds of reasons, and sometimes those reasons just involve things that lie outside their control. Sometimes they just don't realize how serious something might be, or that it's a problem at all. They simply haven't thought their way through the whole thing."

## Projecting the blame

We all know how easy it is to point the finger at someone else when something bad happens. It can be very tough to take full blame for something, especially when the potential consequences are extremely serious. So you need to make it as easy as possible for the person you're interrogating to admit his own culpability. We've found it's very effective in a monologue to convey to the person the notion that whatever it is he did, it's not entirely his fault. So whose fault is it? Society's, the school's, the system's, the government's. Think big—bigger is always easier to defend, because it's more nebulous. If you get explicit, you're putting yourself in harm's way, because it might sound as if you're promising him something, or letting him off the hook. In his interrogation of Lee, Phil placed the blame on the amorphous sphere of "politics":

- "So regardless of all the political stuff, Lee, I can fully understand why you would be attracted to the Foelandian people."

He also suggested that the Foelandians might shoulder some of the blame, but he did it in a way that didn't denigrate anyone Lee might feel an affinity toward:

- "Maybe your Foelandians friends took advantage of you—I don't know, that's not my call, and I'm not going to sit here in judgment of anybody."

## Minimizing the seriousness

To keep the person in short-term thinking mode, it's essential that he not dwell on the potential consequences of his actions. A very effective way to prevent that is to downplay the gravity of the situation. You don't want to dissemble by implying that it's not a problem. But it is possible to convey some sense that it could be worse, and that the situation isn't irreparable, with statements like, "It's not the end of the world," or "It's a fixable problem." You just don't specify what the "fix" is. Phil conveyed that sense to Lee this way:

- "[Nate] was worried that you might think that something could disqualify you, when in reality there's not a whole lot we haven't seen and been able to work through. You know, Nate was saying you're kind of a perfectionist, and the fact is, we live in an imperfect world, Lee. We talk with guys all the time who think they have to be perfect. That's not the way it works."

- "Nate's my friend, too, and of course I don't want to have to deliver any bad news to him. But that's just it, Lee—it doesn't have to be bad news. There's no reason in the world why it has to be bad news. Because whatever it is that's bothering you, you have to understand it can be fixed. It's a fixable problem."

## Socializing the situation

We're all social beings, so your subject needs to feel that he isn't in isolation, or that he's been forsaken. He needs to know that other people have been in the same boat he's in, and we accomplish that by populating the context of the monologue. Here are some examples of how Phil accomplished it with Lee:

- "Lee, please understand that in our world, this is the sort of thing we see all the time. I've worked with people from all walks of life—mothers, fathers, students, government officials, corporate executives—who have found themselves in exactly the same situation we're looking at right now."
- "It's nothing we haven't dealt with before, nothing that would surprise us. I've been doing this for a long time, Lee, and I can tell you, there's not a single problem that's ever come up in this kind of a situation that we haven't been able to work through and fix."
- "I understand that, Nate understands that, everybody understands that."

## Emphasizing the truth

Your subject's frame of mind needs to be focused on telling you the truth, rather than on the action itself. And he needs to be convinced that the *only* way out of the predicament he's in is to be truthful with you. Phil made that point very clear with Lee:

- "What I do know is that this is a fixable problem. But in order to fix it, we need to get everything out on the table so we know what we're dealing with. That's the only way."

Keep in mind, also, that word choice is a critical element in weaving these components into your monologue. You'll recall that in the case of Jan, the pharmacy technician who misappropriated the oxycodone tablets, we referred to our *inquiry* rather than an *investigation*, and we said she *took* the tablets, she didn't *steal* them. Similarly in the monologue that Phil delivered to Lee, note that in his DOG, Phil referred to Lee's work with Horace in an *intelligence-gathering* capacity, rather than in terms of being a *spy*, or *conducting espionage*. He made reference to Lee's Foelandian *friends* rather than to *FIS contacts*. Such harsh language needs to be avoided so the subject stays in short-term thinking mode, and isn't beginning to think about the negative consequences of his actions.

On one occasion, when Michael was working on an espionage case at the Agency, the suspect told Michael that he had been labeled by investigators as a "spy." Michael knew he had to work quickly to reverse the damage created by that harsh language. This simple exchange did the trick:

**Michael:** They called you a *what?*
**Suspect:** They called me a spy.
**Michael:** What's a spy?

**Suspect:** I don't know. I guess someone who sells secrets for money.

**Michael:** You know that's BS in your case, because we all know you were merely sharing information to help promote the global stability that we're all working for.

Yes, it was kind of hokey. But it worked.

It's also important to bear in mind that the use of insulting or offensive language can cause a person to clam up altogether. Michael was once hired by a prominent criminal defense lawyer who was representing a client of Chinese descent. The client was a nuclear physicist employed by a major defense contractor, and he had allegedly provided classified information to Chinese intelligence services. He had been under FBI surveillance for some time, and was photographed and recorded meeting with known Chinese intelligence agents on numerous occasions.

He was brought in for questioning, and for what the FBI fully expected to be a confession, considering the amount of incriminating evidence that had been collected. According to the suspect, when he walked into the interrogation room to be questioned by two FBI agents, one of the agents opened the encounter with the instruction, "Sit over there, Chinaman."

That treatment contrasted sharply with the respectful approach taken by Michael, whose understanding and sincerity had led the suspect to open up to him much more extensively than he had to the FBI. In fact, when he heard that racial slur, the suspect said he told himself, "No matter how much evidence they produce, no matter how obvious my guilt becomes, I will never, never, never give these two agents the satisfaction of obtaining my confession." In the end, the government struck a plea bargain that resulted in no prison time for this nuclear scientist who ultimately confessed to passing secrets to China.

———

## ELEMENTS OF A MONOLOGUE

- Rationalize the action
- Project the blame
- Minimize the seriousness
- Socialize the situation
- Emphasize the truth

Let's say it's Friday night, and you've gone with your significant other to see a movie. Being the good moviegoing citizen you are, you turned your phone off when you were instructed to do so by the zombie/cowboy/warrior in the clever spot following the previews of coming attractions. After the movie, as you're walking out of the theater, you turn your phone back on, and you see you have a missed call and a voicemail from a number you don't recognize. You're curious, so you decide to listen to the voicemail—chatting with your significant other about the movie will have to wait. You tap the button on the voicemail screen, and this is what you hear:

"This is Detective Williams with the State Police. Please call me at this number at your earliest convenience. Thank you."

Your heart starts beating a mile a minute. Why on earth is a State Police detective calling you? You know you haven't done anything wrong. You even turn your phone off whenever you're supposed to. Doesn't matter. Your heart is still racing. *What did I do?* The fact of the matter is, there are any number of perfectly reasonable explanations for the call that have nothing to do with any wrongdoing on your part. Maybe Detective Williams dialed the wrong number. Maybe he was doing fundraising for the families of deceased and disabled police officers. Maybe there was a burglary on your street, and he was calling everyone who lived nearby to see if they'd seen any suspicious activity. Your mind went to none of those places. You were too busy jumping from bleak scenario to bleak scenario. How are you going to explain whatever they think you did wrong to your significant other and your family? Are you going to need a lawyer? You don't even know any lawyers. Except that guy at the gym, but he's an imbecile. Are you going to have to take time off from work? If you do, what should you tell your boss?

By the time you get home, you're frantic. And it's all because of a very simple diagnosis. You've contracted a mind virus.

*Mind virus* is a colloquial term for the psychological discomfort a person feels when he receives information that has potentially negative consequences, causing his mind to race with hypothetical ramifications of the information. We're all vulnerable to them. There's no inoculation that can protect us from them.

The mind virus phenomenon is one that will tend to work to your advantage in an elicitation situation, and you can even use it to great effect when the hypothetical consequences are positive. The way to trigger it is by using implicit, rather than explicit, language.

Let's say you're a school administrator, and you're speaking with a student who, according to three of his classmates, had brought a gun into school the day before. The students didn't report it until today, and a search of his locker and belongings failed to turn up any gun. The most likely scenario, given the information you have, is that the student brought the gun to school yesterday, but took it home at the end of the day and left it there. Still, if he did bring a gun into the school, you need to know.

Now, you clearly can't say to him, "If you tell me, we're not going to expel you." But what you can say is something on the order of, "Our goal here is to get this resolved—to understand why this issue has come up, and to get it worked out." Then you let his mind take that and run with it. Let him put his own spin on what "resolve" means, what "worked out" means. Then, if he does come out and ask what "resolve" means, don't box yourself in. You might respond with something like this:

"Listen, 'resolve' simply means that we need to understand why this happened. Once we understand why this happened, then we can think about next steps. We can't even begin to think about next steps at this point, because we have no idea why it happened. We know what, we know who, but we don't know why. You need to help us understand that. Then we can figure out where to go from there."

The beautiful part is that if the consequences go against him, he understands that it's his fault—it's not your fault, it's not the school's fault, it's not the system's fault. And he came to that understanding without you having to beat him over the head with his mistake.

Phil used precisely the same strategy in his interrogation of Lee. Clearly, he couldn't let Lee off the hook, so he let the mind virus do its thing. When he told Lee that getting everything out on the table was the only way to fix the problem, he left it to Lee to put his own spin on whatever "fix" might mean. When he told him that Nate "knows you can do so much good for so many people, given the opportunity," he let Lee decide whether that meant he still had a future with the Agency. When he suggested that "maybe your Foelandian friends took advantage of you," it was up to Lee to decide where to take that.

It's important to be clear that while the process of building the monologue is, to some extent, a formulaic one, it is not one that allows for any sort of cookie-cutter approach. No doubt, some of the phrases we commonly use are applicable to just about any situation. But what you need to strictly avoid is employing any kind of plug-and-play technique, or creating a monologue that's nothing but an amalgamation of sound bites. You need to customize the monologue to the individual and the situation you're dealing with. That effort begins even before you transition into interrogation mode, by ensuring that you're listening closely and assimilating what the person is saying during the interview. If he mentions in his response to one of your questions that his wife is expecting, or that he was recently laid off, or that money is tight because he has three kids in college, that information can be invaluable in helping you to craft customized rationalization statements that will strike a chord.

It's also essential to be thoroughly informed about the case facts. In Phil's interrogation of Lee, he capitalized on Lee's friendship with Nate. The same strategy holds for any elicitation: The monologue you build needs to be constructed around whatever information you have about the individual.

Suppose you're an office manager, and you've discovered that $50 is missing from the petty cash box. The timing and circumstances are such that it's almost certain that Sally, an assistant bookkeeper, took the money. You know that she's a single mom, and that she's struggling to make ends meet. When you confront her, she denies knowing anything about the missing money. So what you convey to her might go something like this:

"Sally, as I was preparing to sit down to talk to you, one of the things that occurred to me, knowing what I know about you, is why would this happen to her? Why might she do something like this? You know, over the years, I've talked to a lot of people who do things for reasons that nobody can justify, or understand. But what if this is a totally different situation?

For example, I ask myself, what if I were to go home one night, and my son and daughter looked up at me and said, 'Mommy, what's for dinner?' And I'm confronted with the truth: There is no dinner. There's nothing in the refrigerator. There's nothing in the cabinets. There's no money in my purse. There *is* no dinner. Would I do something I normally would never do, because now I have no choice? What if I was forced to make that decision? I'm very lucky, Sally. I don't have to do that. The point I'm trying to make is that if you've been in those kinds of situations, we need to know that. We need to understand that. It still doesn't necessarily turn an unfortunate decision into a good decision, but it helps us understand. Because we all make unfortunate decisions. We make them every day. But what's important here is to help people understand *why* this happened."

Nothing cookie-cutter about that. It speaks directly to Sally's personal situation, and it's presented in a way that will connect with her. Of course, it's not always quite that easy. It's one thing when the issue you're dealing with is $50 missing from petty cash. But what if you were investigating an unspeakable crime? Customizing the monologue in those cases requires a lot of experience. Unless you're in a position like that of a law enforcement officer who is routinely exposed to heinous crimes, or a psychologist who has worked with people who have all sorts of serious problems, it's hard to imagine some of the things we as human beings are capable of. So it can be very difficult in those cases to create a monologue that's more than a collection of standard sound bites. You can rationalize, minimize, and project the blame for anything, but for it to be meaningful it has to be consistent with the gravity and case facts of the situation. There has to be a base of rationalizations and defenses to draw upon in order to make the monologue relevant. So experience and training in those areas become essential.

The same fundamental idea is applicable to other, less intense situations. Let's say you're a human resources manager, and part of your job is to screen and interview job candidates. Over time, you'll develop a sense of what people tend to lie about—how they might falsify their résumés, or embellish their education or skill level. So you'll need to maintain a monologue base, and generate a repository of meaningful rationalizations and other information to draw from during the interview. If, for example, you work for a professional sports franchise, and you find that the candidates who apply for a public relations position tend to grossly exaggerate their list of professional contacts in that sport, you need to be able to manage that. You need to be prepared for that problem to crop up in the interview, because it's critical that you gain an accurate picture of the connectedness of each candidate so you and the hiring manager can make the best hiring decision. If the issue arises, and you find you need to persuade the candidate to come clean on what his real level of connectedness is, it'll be very helpful to have a rationalization to draw upon that will help him out. It might sound something like this:

"You know, what we've found in interviewing for this position is that a lot of people think they have to have some massive database of high-profile contacts in order to even be considered for the job, so they end up going a little over the top in how they portray their own situation. That's perfectly understandable, because there's a lot of misinformation and disinformation out there about what the expectations are. The truth is, that's nowhere near the top of the list of what we're looking for. We already have a robust contact database. The right person for this position is someone we can work with to exploit that database, and add to it over time. We want to be able to provide whatever support is needed, but to do that, it's essential that we have a really accurate picture of what we're working with. Without that, it's very difficult to move forward in this process."

Boom. You just made him see the light.

The process of interviewing and interrogating children must be executed with extreme care. Children sometimes answer questions they don't understand, and sometimes provide answers to questions without realizing they're mistaken. Anyone who deals with children knows that the line between fantasy and reality is often blurred, and what we might consider to be a lie is not a lie in the mind of a child. The monologue must therefore be tailored in a way that takes those factors into account.

Michael was once contracted by a lawyer, whom we'll call "Mr. Jones," to interview a thirteen-year-old girl—let's call her "Paulette"—who claimed to be a victim of severe abuse by members of a satanic cult when she was six years old. It was a particularly disturbing case. According to Paulette, she, along with sixty other children, were subjected to satanic rituals that included rape and torture at the hands of the leader of a satanic cult in California. Some children, Paulette claimed, had been murdered. Mr. Jones was investigating the possibility of filing a class-action lawsuit against the satanic cult, and he saw Paulette as the most credible voice among the children who had allegedly been harmed. Mr. Jones either truly believed Paulette's story, or desperately wanted to believe it. So he hired Michael to interview her, with the expectation that he would find her to be truthful. That finding would greatly strengthen his case.

Going into the interview, Michael knew that he had at least three obstacles to overcome. First, Paulette had been interviewed multiple times by family members, police officers, therapists, and attorneys. Along the way, she had undoubtedly been subjected to leading and suggestive questions, and it likely was becoming more difficult by the day for Paulette to separate fantasy from reality. Was she reading their inadvertent signals and merely telling the interviewers what she believed they wanted to hear? Some of her interviewers may have deliberately distorted the issue for personal notoriety and profit, in light of the potential class-action lawsuit. Second, we know that the longer the span of time between an event and the disclosure of information about that event, the greater the likelihood that there will be problems in determining the truth of the matter. In Paulette's young life, the seven years that elapsed between the event and the disclosure was an eternity. Third, interviewing children is a challenge in any case, but the fact that this case involved topics like satanic rituals, rape, torture, and murder made it extraordinarily sensitive.

Paulette's story was both bizarre and horrific. As Michael listened to her account, he remained objective and nonjudgmental, recognizing that displaying any sort of emotion could influence her responses to his questions. Over the two days he spent with Paulette, he was struck by how strongly she appeared to believe her story. Was her display of credibility the result of her actual experience, or of having told the story repeatedly in a variety of settings, creating what she eventually thought of as a memory that she actually believed to be true? Let's look at an excerpt from the transcript of the interview, in which only the names have been changed:

**Michael:** In your earlier statement, you said you were raped by Mr. X at his apartment in San Francisco.
**Paulette:** I don't know if we had sex because he injected me with something and I can't remember.

**Michael:** Did you see Mr. X stab the little boy with the tire iron in the underwater cave?

**Paulette:** It was Stan.

**Michael:** In your earlier statement, you said it was Mr. X. Was it Stan or was it Mr. X that stabbed the little boy?

**Paulette:** Mr. X.

**Michael:** Why did you say Stan?

**Paulette:** I don't know.

**Michael:** How did you get to the cave?

**Paulette:** We flew in a helicopter to somewhere, I don't know.

**Michael:** Where did the helicopter land?

**Paulette:** In a field and then we rode on a bus to the lake.

**Michael:** You said you read a sign on a locked gate leading to the lake where the cave is located. You said the sign read, "No Trespassing," right?

**Paulette:** Yeah.

**Michael:** You also said earlier that you hadn't learned to read yet when you took that trip. How do you know the sign said "No Trespassing"?

**Paulette:** Once I learned to read, I knew that's what the sign said.

**Michael:** Tell me about how you got to the underwater cave in the lake.

**Paulette:** We [Paulette and two other girls, ages four and six] changed into long T-shirts. They spent a few minutes teaching us how to scuba dive.

**Michael:** How did they teach you?

**Paulette:** We didn't get into the water. We just stood on the shore and they put the scuba gear on us.

[Michael asked Paulette to draw a picture of the scuba gear they supposedly used. In her drawing, the children looked like they were about to be launched into space.]

**Michael:** Do you know how to swim?

**Paulette:** No.

**Michael:** Then what?

**Paulette:** Then we got into a rowboat with one adult and rowed out into the middle of the lake.

**Michael:** Were you wearing life jackets?

**Paulette:** No.

**Michael:** When did you put on the scuba gear?

**Paulette:** We had it on when we got in the boat and we were breathing with our scuba gear on the way in the boat.

**Michael:** When you got to the middle of the lake what happened?

**Paulette:** We all jumped in the water.

**Michael:** Who rowed the boat back to shore if there was only one adult in the boat?

**Paulette:** I guess there must have been two adults then.

**Michael:** Then what happened?

**Paulette:** Me and the youngest girl each took one of his hands and dove down into the water. He had a flashlight.

**Michael:** Then what happened?

**Paulette:** The other girl dove under the water with us and it took us about a minute and a half to reach the cave.

**Michael:** If the adult was holding each of you by the hand and a flashlight, too, how did he swim?

**Paulette:** [Physically demonstrates the adult swimming underwater with both hands.]

**Michael:** Okay. Then what happened?

**Paulette:** We went down about twelve feet and there was a plastic cover that he pulled apart so we could swim into the cave.

**Michael:** Describe the cave for me.

**Paulette:** Well, I don't know. I guess it was one room with a dirt floor and a skylight.

[Michael walks Paulette through her gruesome description of satanic rituals, rape, torture, and murder.]

**Michael:** How did you return from the cave?
**Paulette:** We swam to the surface, but the boat wasn't there, so we all swam to shore.
**Michael:** How did that work exactly?
**Paulette:** He held two of us with each hand and the littlest one swam on her own.

By that point, Paulette's inconsistent statements had made it clear to Michael that she wasn't being truthful. It was time for Michael to switch into interrogation mode, and to begin his monologue.

**Michael:** Paulette, I've listened to your story over the last two days, and it's obvious that something has been bothering you. I know Mr. Jones told you that my job is to know when people are telling the truth and when people are making up a story. I think what's been bothering you is that some of the things you have been telling me aren't completely true. But that's okay, Paulette. I don't want you to worry about that.

You've been telling this story for a long time. If you tell a story long enough, you sometimes begin to believe it yourself. I think a little bit of that happened here. After a while, it just becomes part of who you are. I'm guessing that at first, you probably did this as a game to see how people would react. I don't think you even expected people to believe you at first. But when people believed you, it made it very hard to say you were just playing around. It all started to get very confusing for you, and before you knew it, here I came to talk to you, and this thing got all blown up and out of control.

You know, I almost have to laugh when I think about how crazy people started to get. It is kind of funny when you think about it. Yeah, I think you'd have to agree it got a little nuts, but I blame the adults involved in this, not you. When a lot of what you were saying really didn't make sense, anyone with half a brain should have known you were just playing around. If I was you, I wouldn't feel embarrassed about this because nobody got hurt.

When I was a little kid, I remember trading a neighbor kid a stupid little stick for his toy stagecoach and horses.

**Paulette:** [Laughs]

**Michael:** When I came home, my mom asked me where I got the stagecoach and horses. I told her I found it. She knew I was lying, but I thought if I told her the truth she would make me give the stagecoach back to the neighbor kid. After I finally told her the truth she told me that she understood, but that she thought I had taken advantage of the kid. She wanted me to do the right thing. It was hard, but I gave the stagecoach back, and my mom was proud of me. It's funny that I still remember the good feeling I got from telling the truth and doing the right thing. Just like I did, you can do the right thing and tell the truth, too. I know you can.

Paulette, you're a good person and the last thing I want to do is make you feel bad or feel embarrassed. Trust me, I've been there myself, more than I care to admit. I'm not perfect, either. Do you have erasers on your pencils at school?

**Paulette:** Yeah.

**Michael:** I know. That's why they put erasers on pencils, because they know people make mistakes. I know people will understand, because I understand. Nobody is

## TAILORING YOUR MONOLOGUE FOR CHILDREN

Here are some tips to keep in mind when interviewing or interrogating a child:

- Explain why the interview is taking place, and focus on helping the child feel comfortable and safe.
- Establish that the child understands the difference between telling a lie and telling the truth, and that it's okay to say "I don't know" or "I don't understand."
- Be aware that children might say what they think you want to hear rather than speak honestly.
- Tell stories about yourself when you were growing up. Sharing something you did that you shouldn't have done when you were their age helps them to connect with you and see that you understand what they're going through.
- Ask concrete, simple questions. When using conceptual terms (over/under, up/down, in/out, before/after, today/yesterday/tomorrow), make sure the child understands.
- As a parent, pick your battles. Save your monologue approach for the times when it's really needed—situations like cheating in school, involvement with drugs, or criminal activity. Overuse with matters like whether the child did her homework or cleaned up her room will diminish its effectiveness.
- Avoid lying to your child. That puts you on much firmer ground when you're trying to get him to tell you the truth.

going to get mad at you. Before I leave today, I'll help you talk to Mr. Jones and explain what's going on. I know he'll be pleased that we set the record straight before he files his papers with the court. It might seem a little uncomfortable at first, but you're a brave young lady, and we'll get through this together.

Paulette, let me ask you this: Were you really trying to hurt Mr. X and the others, or were you just playing around?

**Paulette:** Playing around, that's all.

**Michael:** Thanks for that, Paulette. I'm proud of you. It's all going to work out.

Michael and Mr. Jones had their answer. It wasn't the answer that Mr. Jones had hoped for, but he accepted it, and he commended Michael for his success in getting the truth. The lawsuit was never filed.

# 7.
# HOW TO HANDLE RESISTANCE DURING YOUR MONOLOGUE
||||||||||||||||||||||||||||||||||||||||||||||||||||||||

Phil has a hat hanging in his office that's embroidered with the expression, "If your lips are moving, you must be lying." In truth, we're not that cynical. But what we can say without equivocation is that if a person is lying, we don't want his lips moving. That mantra should be emblazoned on your brain in any elicitation situation.

When you transition from interview mode to interrogation mode, you switch from dialogue to monologue for an explicit reason: You want to hear nothing from your subject other than the truth you're seeking, be it an admission, a confession, or simply an accurate account of the facts. Unfortunately, no matter how masterful and captivating your monologue is, you can't assume that the person will sit through it in rapt silence, as if he were watching Hamlet's "To be, or not to be" soliloquy. He's very likely to put up some resistance, and you're going to need to be prepared to handle it.

There are three primary forms of resistance that you can expect to encounter in an elicitation situation: convincing statements, emotion, and denials. Let's take a look at how those types of resistance are demonstrated, and the techniques you can use to overcome them.

## CONVINCING STATEMENTS

Convincing statements are statements that are made to influence or manipulate perception, and they're extraordinarily powerful. Their power lies in the fact that they're either true, or they're irrefutable. Let's go back to Chapter 3, and the case of the missing oxycodone tablets. You've switched into interrogation mode with Jan, the pharmacy technician who, the case facts show, is responsible for the theft. You're well into your monologue when suddenly Jan cuts you off. "Wait a minute," she says, and in the same breath she launches into her argument:

"This doesn't make any sense. I've been working here for six years, and I've never, ever been accused of doing anything wrong. I've trained most of the other techs, and they respect me. I'm just not the type of person who would do something like that. Why would I risk my job for some damn oxycodone?"

Jan wants to persuade you that you're barking up the wrong tree, and her game plan is to accomplish that by painting herself with a halo. Everything she said was either true—she did indeed train most of the other techs, and they do indeed respect her—or irrefutable—whether or not she's the type of person who would do something like that is yet to be determined. Those convincing statements are powerful because they're so, well, *convincing*. You can even imagine yourself saying something like that if *you* were falsely accused of the theft. The difference is that in all likelihood, while you might find yourself making one of these statements during the exchange, your focus would be on making the point that you didn't do it, rather than on coming up with a raft of convincing statements as a means of painting that halo.

So when you hear those statements from Jan, you need to recognize them for what they are, and sap their power by neutralizing them. The way to do that is to simply agree with them: "Jan, listen, you're exactly right—everyone in the store knows how hard you work. I'm always hearing the other techs

## USING AGREEMENT TO NEUTRALIZE CONVINCING STATEMENTS

- By agreeing with Jan, you've conveyed that you have, without question, heard what she just told you.
- Your reaction seems counterintuitive to her, in the sense that her purpose is to put up resistance, and yet you suddenly seem to be on her side. For a moment, she thinks she may have convinced you.
- When you return to your monologue, she's likely thinking, *Oh, my God, it didn't work.*
- The recognition that that tack was ineffective puts her on the spot, and she has to try to figure out what to do now. She may be thinking that giving you at least *some* truthful information has become an option.
- You've disarmed her by taking away one of her most powerful weapons. Absent any others, she's more inclined to listen to what you're saying. Without realizing it, she has just stepped onto the slippery slope of short-term thinking.

say how helpful you are, and you've certainly been very helpful to me over the years."

And then you go right back into your monologue:

"That's why it's so important that we resolve this, so we
can get on with the business of doing what we do so well, and
what so many people depend on us to do. They don't look to
us to sit in judgment of anyone, and none of us should have
any inclination to do that. We just need to figure out why this
happened, and fix it so we can go back to helping people."

Jan recognizes that her game plan didn't pan out the way
she hoped it would. Trying to persuade you by influencing
your perception of her got her nowhere. She has no choice
but to abandon that tack.

## EMOTION

Since Jan has to change her strategy, she may well give emotion
a shot. This might take the form of crying, hitting you with an
outburst of anger, or showing a flare-up of fear or panic. You
certainly don't want to ignore the emotion, but you can't
allow it to steer you away from your approach, either. If Jan
starts crying, you want to acknowledge it, and then overcome
it by making it clear, gently but firmly, that it's not going to
work:

"Jan, I know you're upset. Please understand that's not my
intent—the last thing I want to do is to make this any harder
for you than it has to be. And you also need to understand
that it's not going to fix anything—getting upset isn't going to
do either one of us any good."

And then you go right back to your monologue.

Outbursts of anger or panic can be a little more difficult to
handle, but they're manageable, as long as you keep your cool.
Susan once conducted a routine security reinvestigation of an

Agency employee we'll call "Stella," a woman she had to interview four times because of the deceptive behaviors she exhibited in response to questions about her protection of classified information. Stella, who had referred to Susan as the "bleached blond goddess of torture" after the first three encounters, was having a tough time. These interviews can be difficult under any circumstances due to their inherently invasive nature, but for a person who's trying to withhold information, they're not only difficult, but incredibly draining. By the fourth interview, it was clear to Susan that Stella had engaged in some particularly egregious mishandling of highly classified documents, so she transitioned into elicitation mode. As Susan progressed through her monologue with calm assurances that she had seen this sort of thing many times before with other employees, her tone was caring and sympathetic. It didn't have the desired effect. Stella started screaming at Susan that she had had enough, and that if Susan didn't back off, she was going up to the seventh floor—the floor where the director's suite and other high-level offices are located—and throw herself off the balcony.

Susan was unfazed. "Stella, I know how difficult this must be," she said gently. "But the only way to fix this is to remain calm and levelheaded so that you can help us understand what has happened, and why. That way, it can be resolved, and we can get past it." And she went right back into her monologue.

Just as in the case of neutralizing convincing statements, the message that's conveyed is simple: *It didn't work. You're not going to intimidate me, you're not going to sway me, you're not going to influence me. You're going to have to come up with a different plan, and I'm here to help you do that.*

Although emotion can be difficult to handle, its display isn't necessarily a bad thing. We've found that quite often the confession comes very soon after emotion is exhibited. Emotion, particularly anger and aggression, is often a last resort.

Once you work your way through that, you're just about there. The person realizes there's no use in trying to keep going.

## DENIALS

Remember that mantra we introduced earlier: If the person is lying, we don't want his lips moving. So when resistance surfaces in the form of an attempt to voice a denial, you need to nip it in the bud. As we noted in Chapter 5, it's important to be engaged and attentive throughout your monologue, and one of the benefits of that is that it helps you pick up on any signal that a denial is coming. Quite often, if the person intends to interrupt your monologue with a denial, he'll signal it with a phrase like, "I already told you . . ." or "I'm telling you . . ." That's your cue to do some quick manipulation.

If you get such an indication from Jan that she's going to try to derail you with a denial, or if she beats you to the punch and is able to voice the denial, there are several immediate actions you can take to quash her effort. First, if you want to get a person to stop talking, a very effective way to accomplish that is with one word: the person's name. A fascinating nuance of human communication is that when we hear our name, we have a natural inclination to switch from speaking mode to listening mode, because it's the way people typically get our attention to tell us something—we hear our name, and our ears perk up.

The next step is to use a control phrase, like, "Jan, hold on a second," or "Jan, give me a chance to make this clear." That enables you to gain control of the exchange, and to ease back into your monologue. As always, it needs to be conveyed calmly, and without raising your voice—trying to control the situation by turning up your volume will create a confrontational atmosphere that will only make your job more difficult.

Third, a remarkably effective mechanism to get someone to stop talking is the universal stop sign: You hold up your hand. You do it almost as a gesture of self-defense—you're not extending it out aggressively and shoving it into the person's face, or doing it with attitude. It's a visual amplification of your control phrase, and it's more powerful than you might imagine. The reason is that this is a verbal battle, and when you get the person to stop talking, you've taken away his weapon. In medieval times, it was a clash of swords; in the Wild West, it was a gunfight. The knight whose sword was stricken from his hand, the cowboy whose gun was emptied of its bullets, suddenly had no choice but to raise his arms in surrender. He was helpless. That same sense of helplessness can overwhelm a person in a verbal battle if he's unable to speak. It becomes a one-sided fight.

Several investigators from a sheriff's department in California who had undergone our training several years ago later got in touch with us to share the story of how they had recently broken up a gang-related theft ring. They did it by getting one of the gang members, whom we'll call "Carl," to admit that the gang had broken into a warehouse and stolen over $100,000 worth of desktop computer systems.

The investigators' supervisor had contended that it would be pointless to interview Carl, because he was one of the more hardened gang members, and there was no way he was going to talk. The supervisor relented when the investigators insisted that it was worth a shot. After they got the confession, the stunned supervisor wanted to know how they did it. They went back into the interview room and asked Carl what prompted him to confess.

"As soon as I saw your hand come up, and you wouldn't

let me lie to you," Carl said, "I knew it was game over." Without being able to say anything, it was like he had brought a knife to a gunfight. He had no chance.

Resistance varies not only in the form it takes, but in the timing of its appearance. Often, it appears before the engagement even begins. If a person has made up his mind that he's going to resist the process, whether it's a screening interview, a criminal questioning, or some other encounter, his aim will likely be to try to delay or control the situation. That was certainly the case with a senior executive with a Fortune 500 company, whom we'll call "Norman."

Early in his career at the Agency, Phil was assigned to a case related to the selection of Norman's company for a government contract. The sensitive nature of the work that was to be performed under the contract was such that several executives within the company, including Norman, were required to obtain security clearances. The problem in Norman's case was that his background investigation had revealed that he had a foreign associate whom he had not disclosed to the government as required. It was a serious situation: Norman had lied on a government form about his association with a foreign national. Phil's job was to get Norman to acknowledge the association, ascertain the nature of the relationship, and determine why Norman had failed to disclose it.

A neutral observer could have been forgiven for seeing the matchup as grossly unbalanced. Phil, young and relatively inexperienced, was up against this much older, seasoned executive, who was no doubt used to issuing directives and having them followed. Asserting his control in any business encounter was second nature. Phil knew the moment Norman entered the room that he had his hands full.

Phil introduced himself, and asked Norman to have a seat.

With a silent, dismissive glance, Norman turned and spotted a hanger on a hook on the back of the door. He walked slowly back toward the door, making an elaborate, deliberate effort of taking off his suit coat, hanging it up, and finally sitting down. He looked at Phil. "I don't have a lot of time for this," Norman said, in stark contraposition to his plodding, protracted entrance.

Norman had obviously elected to take an adversarial approach to the engagement with Phil, and to pursue that approach with what we call an "access control" strategy. His aim was to control Phil's access to him by delaying it: The less time Phil had to work with Norman, the reasoning went, the lower his chances for success. That told Phil that Norman's level of concern was extremely high. He was probably scared to death.

Phil knew it was highly likely that Norman's situation involved one of two scenarios: The undisclosed foreign associate was either a woman with whom he was romantically involved, or an international business contact. He also knew that given Norman's high level of concern, it was more likely the former: Norman was married, and the idea of having to acknowledge that he had a foreign girlfriend was more consistent with his behavior than that of simply having to identify a foreign business associate. Phil was prepared to go down both paths, but he picked the girlfriend scenario first.

The problem in this scenario wasn't that Norman was married and had a foreign girlfriend—it was that he had failed to be up front about it, and to disclose it. Phil was well equipped with the tools he needed to address that situation, and to get the truth. His monologue was classic:

"Norman, first of all, it's important to understand that this sort of thing happens a lot. And when I say, 'a lot,' I don't mean just in terms of the number of people we see in this situation. I also mean it in terms of it being across the board, regardless of how high or low the person falls on the org chart. The fact is, there's no one who's immune from this situation—it's a human issue, a relationship issue, and it's a very difficult issue for people to talk about. Believe it or not, we talk to people who are willing to jeopardize their positions, and avoid telling us about the situation, because of their assumption that we're going to begin to make judgments that we're not even legally allowed to make. We're in absolutely no position to make a moral judgment, Norman—it's none of our business. What we do have to understand are the counterintelligence implications. And let me tell you, very rarely in situations like this is there a counterintelligence issue. I'll tell you, if I was in Las Vegas, I'd give at least eighty percent odds that whatever that person sitting there is worried about, he has no reason to be worried about it."

Norman was listening intently, processing what he was hearing. Phil's calming, sympathetic voice, and his compassionate tone, provided a source of comfort.

"Listen, I'm not accusing you of anything, Norman. I'm just trying to sort these things out. If the director of the CIA were to come in here right now and ask me what I know for sure about this situation, I have to tell you, the one thing I know for sure is that as this issue has surfaced, there's something on your mind that's bothering you."

That was Phil's means of testing the water—if he got no resistance to that statement, he'd know two things: First, that he was right about the girlfriend. And second, that he was going to get a confession. If Norman didn't resist the premise that he was concealing something, it was pretty much all over.

Norman slowly nodded. "Yeah," he said.

"Tell me what's bothering you, Norman. Let's clear this up so we can finish up the clearance process," Phil said reassuringly. Norman told Phil about the foreign girlfriend.

## TYPES OF RESISTANCE

- Convincing statements
- Emotion
- Denials

## QUASHING DENIALS

- Use the person's first name
- Articulate a control phrase
- Hold up your hand

Phil, despite his youth and relative inexperience, and Norman's sophistication and well-honed situational management skills, had accomplished his task. The fact that Norman was so completely outgunned was something Phil was still trying to wrap his head around. He knew it wasn't so much him, but rather the power of this emerging process, that yielded the successful outcome. He was awed by it. To this day, that awe has yet to subside.

In the end, Norman obtained his security clearance. That meant far more to Phil than winning the round did.

# 8.

# GOING FOR THE GOLD: COLLECTING NUGGETS OF INFORMATION

||||||||||||||||||||||||||||||||||||

As you proceed with your monologue in your interrogation of Jan, at some point it'll be time to check your progress—you'll need to evaluate where you stand in your quest to persuade Jan to admit that she stole the missing oxycodone. The best time to do that is when you see some sign of buy-in, some indication of agreement with what you've been conveying to her in your monologue. This sign may come in the form of a nonverbal indicator—she might nod her head in agreement when you tell her that the only way to resolve the matter is to get all the facts onto the table. Or it might come verbally—she may agree with a rationalization or minimization statement with an acknowledgment like, "Yeah, things have been tough lately," or "You're right, I'm not a bad person."

Now, how should you phrase your progress check? Suppose you were to simply put it this way:

"Okay, Jan, tell me: Did you take the oxycodone?"

There's a problem with that, and it's a critical one. The message you just sent her is that you still don't know whether she took it or not, and that she still has a chance to convince you that she didn't take it. What she hears is that she can still fight, and she can still win.

Instead of hitting her with the "did you do it" question then, you want to convey it in the form of a *presumptive* question. A presumptive question is exactly what it sounds like—it presumes something related to the matter under discussion or investigation. In this case, your presumptive question might be, "Jan, where is the oxycodone now?" or "Jan, how much of the oxycodone do you still have?"

When she hears that, there are two paths Jan can take. One path is to immediately respond with resistance, in which case you'll need to go right back into your monologue. The other path takes you to your desired destination: the truth. In that case, you go straight into the information collection phase of your interrogation.

The first thing to keep in mind is that it's essential to refrain from any inclination to chastise or penalize Jan. If she says something like, "I'm really sorry, I shouldn't have done it," you'll need to combat any urge to dump on her with a retort like, "Jan, I knew you did it," or "Jan, why didn't you save us both a lot of time and tell me that before?" As you begin your information collection, it's vitally important for Jan to feel good about the path she's chosen, so that she'll be inclined to continue to share truthful information with you.

Your focus, then, needs to be on rewarding Jan for her decision, and we've found that a simple thank-you is a very powerful reward: "Jan, thank you for that. That took a lot of courage." You'll also need to squash any urge to bask in your victory—far from haughty, your tone should be sympathetic: "I know that was very difficult, but you did the right thing." A defense lawyer might claim otherwise, but it's very difficult to argue that telling the truth isn't the right thing to do. In any case, you don't want her head to go there. You want to keep her in short-term thinking mode, and minimization is a useful tool here: "It's not the end of the world, Jan. The sun will come up tomorrow, just as it always has."

The concept of reward in an elicitation situation warrants further elaboration, simply because its expression is so essential in fostering the person's willingness to continue to share truthful information with you. Sometimes the extent of the information that people share when they feel they're being rewarded for it surprises even us.

Not long ago, Susan was called in to conduct a screening interview of a job candidate we'll call "Harriet." As a self-employed contractor, Harriet had moved between employers fairly frequently, so she had undergone employment interviews with HR personnel on a regular basis over the years. Harriet had always made it through those interviews with no problem, so Susan expected the interview with her to go fairly smoothly. It didn't. Susan learned that Harriet had been fired from a couple of jobs because she had trouble getting up in the morning. Harriet initially claimed it was because she liked to watch TV late into the night, but later admitted it was related to her abuse of alcohol and drugs. She went on to admit that several years earlier, she had become so addicted to crack cocaine, her aunt reported her to social services for neglecting her children. Harriet further acknowledged that she still used marijuana and cocaine when she got frustrated. When Susan asked her where she got her cocaine, she responded that she could go to any city in the country and identify a dealer on the street. She added that about a year earlier, she had been shot at by a rival dealer in the middle of a drug buy. She unloaded all of that in an interview that lasted less than an hour.

When it was all over, Susan asked Harriet why she felt comfortable sharing that information with her, when none of it ever came out in any of her previous HR interviews. Harriet explained that every other HR department she'd ever gone through would ask her if she had a problem with alcohol or drugs, she'd say "no," and it was left at that. Harriet told Susan that when she pursued the matter beyond the initial denial, she did it in a way that made her feel better about herself as she gave her progressively more information. And she said it really meant a lot to her that Susan went so far as to thank her for her honesty. It seems the pleasure of hearing a simple thank-you can be kind of addictive in its own right.

At the same time, we've found that a thank-you isn't the only powerful means of rewarding cooperative behavior. Sometimes a little creativity in playing to your audience can go a long way.

Susan once conducted a screening interview with a former special operations officer we'll call "Kevin," who had held a high-level security clearance for a number of years. In the course of the interview, it became clear to Susan that Kevin enjoyed his alcohol quite a bit. It also became clear that he was having some difficulty with the standard questions regarding sexual deviancy. Kevin had displayed a cluster of deceptive behaviors in response to those questions, so Susan had to transition to interrogation mode to get to the bottom of the sexual deviancy issue. Kevin eventually admitted to having engaged in inappropriate sexual behavior on a number of occasions when he had been drinking, and Susan rewarded those admissions by playing to Kevin's machismo.

Susan's brilliance as an interviewer and interrogator is matched only by her brilliance as an actress. It was time to play a role—one that needed to be pulled off with impeccable timing and absolute believability.

"What sorts of things have you done?" Susan asked. "I mean, what would your wife say is the worst thing you've ever done when you were drinking?"

Kevin paused. "Well . . . I'm not comfortable sharing that with you right now," he said. "I'm really not comfortable talking about it."

"Oh, come on, Kevin," Susan said encouragingly. "You can't tell me anything I haven't heard before."

Kevin relented. Susan was wrong. She genuinely thought she'd heard it all. It turned out she hadn't.

"Well," Kevin fumbled, "actually, my wife doesn't know about this. If she did, she'd kill me. There's this bar I go to. Sometimes when I'm there, I get up on the bar, drop my pants, and make funny shadow shapes with my penis."

Unfortunately, in this job there's no such thing as "too much information." But Susan didn't flinch. Her nonchalance made it appear that she was thinking, *If one more guy tells me today that he drops his trousers at a bar and makes funny shadow shapes with his penis, I'm going to start to wonder.* The interview concluded shortly after that, with the nonadversarial nature of the encounter undamaged.

"Okay, so what's the next step?" Kevin asked, as Susan gathered her things to leave.

"You should be hearing from us within a week to ten days," Susan said. She had gotten the information she needed to determine Kevin's suitability to hold a sensitive position. And Kevin left with his dignity intact.


Now that Jan has chosen the confession path, your next task is to conduct a debriefing. Your first inclination might well be to drill down on her theft of the oxycodone. Resist that inclination—you can get to that later. She's in short-term thinking mode, so you need to capitalize on that by taking a lateral approach to determine whether you're looking at a problem that's bigger than the theft of the missing oxycodone:

"Jan, I appreciate this. I know it was difficult. But trust me, it's not the end of the world. Let me ask you, Jan, what other times has something like this happened?"

Let's say that in response to your question, Jan, visibly upset that she's in this predicament, summons the courage to admit that she once slipped a few Vicodin tablets into her pocket. What that tells you is that Jan had additional information that she didn't want to share with you, so it follows that she may well have more information that she wants to withhold. To deal with that, think of the Vicodin admission as what we call a "cliff moment." What Jan may have been thinking was, "Okay, I can tell her about the oxycodone and the Vicodin, but I can't tell her about this and this and this, because if I told her all of that, there's no way I'd be able to keep my job." It's like she's standing on the edge of a cliff, and if she takes one more step, she's gone.

Your job is to explore what's in the ravine on the other side of the cliff. So when Jan tells you about the Vicodin, you acknowledge it, reward her, and keep right on going as if she never even said it. The two most important words in this information collection process are "what else." Think of each subsequent admission as having come to another cliff, and keep exploring what's on the other side. If she exhibits deceptive behavior, you go right back into the monologue. If she admits to something else, you reward. Then you keep going until she says there is nothing else, and she shows no signs of deceptive behavior. With each admission, remember to avoid a deep dive into any one issue. Your best bet is to aim for little nuggets of information, so it doesn't appear that you're asking for a big data dump and an emotionally draining confession. Then, when you have all those nuggets and it's time for your deep dive, don't go back to the beginning—start with the most recent admission first. That's likely the most serious matter, because it's the one she tried hardest to conceal.

Keep in mind as you're collecting those nuggets how

essential it is to remain engaged. As we pointed out in Chapter 6, engaging the person you're interrogating is a vital element in coming across as sincere, which will in turn help you in your effort to persuade the person to share the information you're seeking. But we should make it clear that it's equally important to be engaged from the standpoint of ensuring that you don't miss any of those nuggets that are coming at you.

Susan once did a screening interview with a job candidate we'll call "Marvin," who mentioned during the interview that he had graduated from high school six years earlier. That information typically wouldn't be particularly consequential during an interview of this type, so if the interviewer isn't acutely engaged, something like that can easily become buried under the mental pile of consequential information that's collected over the course of the interview. In this case, when Susan raised the topic of drug use, Marvin admitted to using cocaine five years earlier. For the reasons we've explained, Susan didn't drill down on that admission—it was like she had never even heard it. She proceeded with her line of questioning to determine what other drugs Marvin might have used, and what other times he used them. When she was satisfied that there were no other cliffs to approach, Susan went back to the cocaine admission to drill down on that. When she asked about the circumstances, Marvin said he and some buddies on his high school hockey team had used cocaine at a five-year class reunion. Oops. Marvin didn't realize he had goofed up until Susan called him on it.

"OK, help me understand this, Marvin," Susan said, with no hint of remonstration in her voice. "Earlier you said it was five years ago that you last used cocaine. You also said you graduated from high school six years ago. If you used the cocaine at a five-year class reunion, can you clarify the timeline for me?"

Marvin knew there was no way out. He apologized, and

admitted that it wasn't five years earlier, after all. It turned out he had actually last used cocaine about two months earlier. If Susan hadn't been engaged enough to have caught the seemingly insignificant fact that Marvin had graduated from high school six years earlier, she would have been beaten on the drug question.

Speaking of cliff moments, if you happen to be a woman, and you've ever found yourself in the position of needing to purchase a new car, you probably know what it feels like to want to take a leap off the nearest cliff. It can be an outrageously frustrating experience when unscrupulous salesmen do their best to capitalize on a situation in which they perceive themselves as having the upper hand. The trick is to turn the tables, and to use those cliff moments to your advantage.

Not long ago, Susan was in the market for a new car. Her experience at the first dealership she went to gave her a sense of what she was up against. She had seen an ad for a special sale on a particular model at this dealership—every car on the lot that was this particular model was being sold at one very attractive, low price. When Susan arrived at the dealership, the salesman took her to a lot where all of the cars had been damaged by a recent hail storm—some worse than others. That was odd, Susan thought, because the ad didn't say anything about hail damage. So she asked the salesman if those were the only cars that were included in the sale.

"Oh, no," the salesman replied. "There are others. Did you want to see those?"

"Not anymore," Susan said. And she left.

The next dealership Susan went to played the guilt card, which it apparently found to be especially effective with women. After a test drive, the salesman suggested to Susan that she take the car home and drive it for a couple of days. Susan resisted, but the salesman was adamant. "Take it," he said. "Once you've really experienced it, you're not going to want to bring it back."

Susan relented. She left her car at the dealership, and drove the new car home. When she brought it back the next day, the salesman was delighted to see her.

"Let me get someone to help you move the things from your old car into this one," he said matter-of-factly. When Susan told him to hold on, that she had decided not to buy it, the chipper expression on the salesman's face turned to hurt, as if Susan had taken advantage of him. It didn't work. Susan told him, in not so many words, to stick his guilt card back in his deck.

After a couple of additional unpleasant experiences that went nowhere, Susan resolved to go to the next dealership fully prepared so she could nip the games in the bud. She immersed herself in research—she decided what make and model she wanted, determined which dealership received the highest online ratings from customers, figured out what extras she needed and what she didn't, and learned how sales commissions work at car dealerships.

When she arrived at the dealership, she was immediately approached by a salesman we'll call "Steve." Susan told Steve she had her eye on a particular car, and said the first thing she wanted to do was find out what she could get for her trade-in. Steve inspected Susan's car, fumbled at his computer, and came up with an answer. "Ten thousand," he said.

That was the first cliff moment of the encounter. That may or may not have been the most Susan would be able to get for her car, so she had to test it. It was as if she never heard Steve's answer.

"For a car with mileage that low and that's in such good shape, what's the most you can give me on the trade-in?" Susan asked. Steve hesitated.

"We've got a phenomenal reputation for paying top dollar on trade-ins," he said. "You wouldn't be able to find another dealership that would offer you more than that."

Those convincing statements told Susan that there was a possibility, perhaps a probability, that she'd be able to get more. It was time to go into what you might think of as a mini-monologue to persuade Steve to raise the offer.

"Steve, I really don't want to waste your time, and I certainly don't want to offend you," she began. "But I'm working within a budget, so I have to work with you to get this within a certain range. I've heard you guys give great deals—that's the reason I came here. A friend of mine was saying you're willing to work with people, so I just need you to know, whatever you can do to get me a little more on that trade-in would really be helpful."

Steve could see this wasn't going to be as easy as he thought it was going to be. Susan eventually got him to commit to $12,500 for the trade-in, so it was time to find out how much she could get Steve to chop off the sticker price of the new car. The scene replayed itself with a couple more cliff moments, and when it was all over, Susan had gotten enough off the sticker price to match some of the best deals she had come across in her research.

At that point, Steve likely wanted to salvage as much as he could out of the deal, so he told Susan about a special warranty, maintenance, and roadside assistance package that he highly recommended she purchase.

"Especially as a woman," Steve said, "the last thing you want is to be broken down in some unsafe area because the car wasn't properly serviced," Steve said. "This package will ensure that the car is always as dependable as it is when you drive it off the lot. It would make me feel better if I knew you were safe in the car I sold you. It's renewed annually, so if you decide after a year that you don't need it, you can cancel it."

Susan let Steve's "especially as a woman" insult go. But not without messing with him a little.

"If I buy the package for the first year, you get a commission, right?" Susan asked. Steve seemed startled by the question.

"Well, yeah," he said.

"And if I cancel it after a year, you still get the commission?"

Steve paused. He was probably thinking, *Note to self: Don't make a beeline to every blonde who walks in the door.* "Yes," he said, recognizing that his "It would make me feel better" line made him look like kind of a jerk. Susan declined the package. And she walked out with a great deal.

# 9.

# CRAFTING A SINCERE, EMPATHETIC MONOLOGUE: FICTION AS AN OPTION

|||||||||||||||||||||||||||||||||||||||||||||||||

When Phil told Lee, the translator at the World Cup who confessed to having been recruited by the FIS, that he had always longed to visit Foeland and meet the Foelandian people, that was completely fictitious. But it was a very effective means of demonstrating sincerity and empathy, vital components of a successful elicitation.

Now, let us make something very clear right up front: The use of fiction in any interview or interrogation situation must lie within some very strict parameters. We use it *solely* as a mechanism to convey sincerity and empathy, with the objective of raising the person's level of comfort in sharing information with us. It is essential that you *never* stray beyond that boundary. Trying to bluff the person, for example, can backfire, big-time. If you tell the person that you have a witness who saw him commit the act under investigation, he can beat you with one word: "Who?" The moment you hesitate in responding, or refuse to respond, the person will feel like you're out to get him, and that will create an adversarial situation that will make your job much more difficult. One clarification here: Understand that there's a huge difference between a *bluff* and a *bait*. A bait question is a hypothetical question that's designed to trigger that mind virus we talked about in Chapter 6, and we use this question type quite regularly, to very positive effect. We typically begin a bait question with the phrase "Is there any reason," as in, "Is there any reason one of your coworkers would tell us that she saw you at Dan's computer that day?" It's a very fair question, because the truthful person can respond to it with no problem. The deceptive person has to process it, and that delay will be very telling.

It's also absolutely essential that you never distort the facts of the matter under investigation. When you employ minimization in the monologue, for example, you can't lead the person to believe that what he did isn't a crime, when you don't know that to be the case. And you can't make promises you can't keep. Ensuring the person of a particular outcome if he confesses is off limits.

With all of that understood, we can tell you that Michael demonstrated the efficacy of incorporating fiction in a monologue at the very outset of his career as an interrogator.

The year was 1975, and Michael had just been honorably discharged from the United States Army after serving as a military police platoon leader and detachment commander in South Korea. He found himself in Chicago, working on his Master of Science degree in Detection of Deception. The training was intense, and extraordinarily stressful—under the watchful eyes of seasoned instructors, Michael and his fellow students performed live interviews and interrogations. The following morning, the instructors pulled no punches as they critiqued the previous day's "performances."

It was under those trying circumstances that Michael was briefed on the case facts for his first formal interview and possible interrogation of his civilian life. A young woman we'll call "Donna," who was working as a clerk at a Chicago pharmacy, was suspected of embezzling nearly $30,000 over a twelve-month period. The investigation revealed that the young woman's mother was suffering from cancer. Because her family had no medical insurance, the medical costs of her treatment were growing at an alarming rate, and the family had fallen deeply into debt. That was music to Michael's ears—not that the family was having severe financial problems, of course, but rather because Michael instantly recognized and, more important, understood Donna's motive for stealing. If ever someone could justify breaking the law, stealing money to save your mother's life is probably as justifiable as it gets.

Knowing full well that he would face the gauntlet of savvy instructors the following morning, Michael was highly motivated to make a strong first impression. In his interview with Donna, who had been unsuccessfully interrogated by several store security officers a day earlier, Michael decided to take a somewhat unorthodox approach with his switch into interrogation mode.

**Michael:** Donna, I know this is going to sound crazy, but I wish I were you right now.

**Donna:** Why would you want to be me right now? I've just been accused of stealing thirty thousand dollars!

**Michael:** Donna, that's fair, but let me explain. I am about to share with you something that I have only shared with a handful of people during my life. As a matter of fact, none of my colleagues here are even aware of what I am about to tell you.

After a long, dramatic pause, Michael resumed his monologue in a hushed tone.

**Michael:** My mother died giving birth to me. [Another
dramatic pause, and Michael is beginning to tear up.]
You can only imagine what birthdays are like for me.
Not a day goes by that I don't think about the sacrifice
my mother made bringing me into this world. Not a day
goes by that I don't think about the gift of life she gave
to me or how much I wish she was still alive. I never
experienced her loving touch, her proud gaze, her voice,
her laughter. The little bit I know about my mother is
what my father has told me, but he doesn't like to talk
about it. It's almost as if he has held me responsible for
her death all these years. I can deal with that. What I
can't deal with is that I never had the chance to tell my
mom, "I love you."

[Michael struggles to regain his composure, and continues.]

**Michael:** Now, I'd be the first person to tell you that
taking money that doesn't belong to you isn't right. But
if anyone understands why this thing happened, it's
me.

**Donna:** But I . . .

[Anticipating that Donna is going to make a denial,
Michael holds up his hand.]

**Michael:** Donna, hang on for a second, please. I know
about your mother's illness, and I am so sorry about
that. The difference between you and me is that you've
had twenty-four years to love your mother and to feel
your mother's love. In many ways, potentially losing

her now is far harder to deal with than what I experienced. You have the memories, and I don't.

At that point, Donna started to cry. It was a strong indication that what Michael was saying was beginning to resonate.

**Michael:** Donna, what I'm trying to say here is you had the chance to help your mother, and I never did have that chance to help my mother. That's what I meant when I told you I wish I were you right now. I know about the hundred sixty-five thousand dollars medical debt, and the financial pressure you and your mother are under as you fight to keep her alive. This has to be a living nightmare for both of you. I know it's just you and your mother who are facing this together, and how close the two of you are. I know you must feel alone and helpless. Donna, I think it's fate that has brought the two of us together this morning, because of what the two of us share. If anybody understands what you are going through, it's me. But I can't do this alone. I need you to work with me. I need your help. We really need to put this behind you so you can move forward, move on with your life. You're only twenty-four, and you can have a bright future. I know you can. I know you will.
**Donna:** [Crying] I don't know, I don't know, I don't know. This is so hard.
**Michael:** Believe me, Donna, I know it's hard. You're a good person who made a mistake. You have to give yourself a break. You've been carrying a very heavy burden for a long, long time. I understand that, people will understand that. Nobody's perfect. Not me, not your mother, nobody. You need to understand that. I think you are being so hard on yourself right now. I know

your mother is proud of you, and she will continue to be proud of you when this is over. But sometimes, good people do bad things. Donna, if your mother was here, don't you think she'd want you to tell the truth?

**Donna:** I know she would.

**Michael:** That's right, Donna, and I'm not surprised to hear you say that. Your mom is right, and you know she's right. It sounds like you have a good mom. I know she raised you to do the right thing, and that's what you need to do now—tell the truth, Donna. You're a good person, and don't let anyone tell you otherwise.

Michael sensed it was time to evaluate his progress with a presumptive question.

**Michael:** Donna, tell me, did you take the money to spend on frivolous things like clothes and jewelry, or did you take the money to help your mother?

**Donna:** [Sobbing, saying nothing as she contemplates whether to confess.]

**Michael:** Donna, come on, work with me, work with me. You need to release this so it will be over. I know it's hard. Like I said, people make mistakes all the time. It's the good people who own up to it. That's what shows someone's true character. We all understand why this thing happened. All you were trying to do was to help your mother. It was for your mother, wasn't it?

**Donna:** [Nods her head in a "yes" motion.]

**Michael:** It's okay, Donna. It's okay. We'll get through this thing.

**Donna:** I'm so sorry, I'm so sorry, I'm so sorry, I'm so sorry. O Lord, help me . . .

**Michael:** I know you are. It's obvious you're sorry. It's obvious that you care. I'm so proud of you, Donna, that you had the courage to own up to it. It's not easy to do. We'll get through this together.

It was time to begin the information collection phase of the interrogation.

**Michael:** Let's talk a little bit about how this all happened, Donna. What would be the largest amount of money you ever took at one time?

Donna went on to share the full details of her embezzlement with Michael. What she didn't know was that as she was speaking, Michael's mother was teaching ages five to thirteen in a one-room schoolhouse, miles from nowhere on the plains of Nebraska. She lived for another twenty-nine years after that interrogation.

What Michael didn't know at the time was that five years later he would be one of the savvy instructors in the gauntlet that critiqued students the morning after their interviews. One of those students was Phil Houston, a young CIA security officer whom the Agency sent to Chicago for training. To this day, Phil is fond of reminding Michael of the supposed mistreatment he suffered under the "arrogant and condescending" tutelage of Michael and his fellow instructors.

# 10.
# DO NO HARM
||||||||||||||||||||||

A couple of years ago, Phil and Michael were on the premises of a client, a boutique construction company that builds customized homes and offices. They had been called in by the company's director of security, whom we'll call "Sandy," to question an employee who was suspected of stealing high-value stone and other materials from several of the company's construction sites. It wasn't just a case of random pilfering—the losses were substantial, and there appeared to be a coordinated effort behind the thievery.

The suspect employee, whom we'll call "Jake," had adamantly denied any involvement in the theft of the materials. Phil and Michael met with him, and within about six hours he had not only admitted to stealing thousands of dollars worth of materials in the two years since he'd been hired, but he identified nearly a dozen other employees he had worked with to pull off the thefts. When Phil and Michael reported all of this to Sandy, she was torn between being glad to have the information, and being bummed that almost all of the company's workers would have to be let go. Her immediate concern was Jake. It was late in the day on Friday, and she knew she wouldn't be able to complete all the documentation to have Jake fired until Monday. But under the circumstances, she had to get Jake's keys, badge, and company-owned devices, and escort him off the premises, immediately.

"Would you guys mind handling that?" Sandy asked.

Now, Jake was a formidable presence. He was about six-four, weighed about two-fifty, and had the build of a linebacker. Phil and Michael could picture him sticking a two-hundred-pound marble slab under his arm and walking out with it. They turned and looked at each other.

"I'm not telling him," Phil said. "You tell him."

"Yeah, right," Michael scoffed. "There's no way. *You* tell him."

"Great," Sandy said with a sigh.

Phil smiled. "We're just messing with you," he said. "We'll take care of it."

They went back to the room where they had questioned Jake, and joined him at the small conference table. Phil took the lead.

"Jake, look, first, and most importantly, we appreciate the way you've handled this situation. You've done the right thing. It's not the easy thing, by any stretch of the imagination, but it's the right thing."

Time to plant the mind virus. Jake needed to have some notion that he might survive this because he's done the right thing.

"We have no idea what the outcome of all this will be, because it's not our job to make a decision about what happens here. Our job is just to figure out what the facts are, and to convey your level of cooperation—you've been extraordinarily cooperative with us, and we appreciate that. Unfortunately, as you might expect, this is going to take some time to sort out. As a result, what we've been asked to do is just to convey to you that you should go home and take it easy. Unfortunately, apparently the rules are that we need to hold on to your keys and badge, and anything else that belongs to the company. I know it's been a really tough day, so just take it easy over the weekend. The company will be in touch with you on Monday to sort all of this out. I'm really sorry to have to hold on to your stuff in the meantime."

"No, I understand," Jake said. "Here you go." He wasn't happy, but he did it.

Phil and Michael walked Jake out to the employee parking lot, which was gated. As Jake got in his car, Phil and Michael went over to the gate—since Jake no longer had his badge, they had to key in the code to open it. The gate started to swing open, and as Jake approached it, he slowed and his window started to come down. That wasn't good. The same thought overtook Phil and Michael simultaneously: *He's got a gun.*

The car stopped, and Jake looked up at them. No gun.

"I just wanted to say it was really a pleasure meeting you guys," he said. "I really wish I'd met you under different circumstances, but it was a real pleasure, and I appreciate it." He stuck his hand out of the window and shook hands with both of them, and drove off. Jake was fired on Monday, and the company hasn't heard from him since.

The takeaway here has to do with a precept that we've borrowed from the medical profession: Do no harm. The employee was fired, but it was done in a way that preserved some equity in his relationship with the employer. You don't have to hear too many stories of a bitter ex-employee returning the next day with an assault weapon and a few hundred rounds of ammunition to appreciate how essential that equity is. In this case, Phil and Michael not only had to get Jake to tell them something he desperately wanted to withhold, but they had to get him to hand over items he certainly didn't want to lose. They used precisely the same methodology to influence Jake in both instances.

It worked because of the way Jake was treated. There was no admonishment, no beating him down to create an adversarial environment. Having to tell somebody else what you've done wrong is a lousy situation to be in, and it makes you feel pretty low. But Jake likely felt that he had been treated fairly, and that under the circumstances he couldn't have been treated any better. He might even have felt that he was treated better than he probably deserved.

One of the most essential elements of the mantra to do no harm is the avoidance of sitting in judgment of anyone. The simple fact is that no good can come from being judgmental of a person in an interrogation situation—in fact, it can severely harm the process. When you're judging someone, you're necessarily displaying a bias, and bias can only have a negative impact on your ability to get the truth. Of course, we're all human, and sometimes we have a natural inclination to judge people who mess up. One of the best ways we've found to fight that inclination is to remember a fundamental verity in life: Sometimes good people do stupid things.

Remembering that verity has helped us on countless occasions over the years, as it did one day when Phil was serving as chief of security at the CIA's primary training facility, known as The Farm. That particular assignment was one of the most critical of Phil's career—the day-to-day activity at The Farm included training for some of the Agency's most sensitive operations, so security was always an especially serious concern. Individuals entrusted with access to The Farm had to be absolutely beyond reproach.

One afternoon, Phil was approached by a female employee who reported a disturbing incident. She told Phil that she had left her purse in a secure area when she went to lunch, and when she returned she found that $40 had been taken from it.

The only other person who had access to that particular area at the time was an employee we'll call "Ronald," so it appeared that Ronald had some explaining to do. It would have been a bad situation in any working environment, but in this one, where practically all of the information retained on site was highly classified, it was dire. If Ronald was capable of stealing money from a colleague's purse, what else might he be capable of stealing?

Phil called Ronald to his office, and conveyed to him what the woman had reported. Ronald's response was somewhat peculiar. Rather than address the topic that Phil had raised, he asked Phil to come with him to the parking lot so he could show him something. Phil had no intention of walking out to the parking lot with Ronald, and when Ronald recognized that, he told Phil what he had wanted him to see: The trunk of his car was filled with Bibles, which he distributed to people on behalf of his church. It was Ronald's way of telling Phil that he was not the type of person who would steal money from a colleague's purse.

What Ronald didn't take into account was that Phil would never allow this good-hearted community service to sway him. Any bias he might have in favor of someone who would perform such an admirable service had to be managed as part of the process of ascertaining the truth of the matter. But what was equally true was that Phil had to manage any bias he might have *against* a trusted employee who would steal his colleague's money. Such a bias could easily cause him to be judgmental of Ronald's actions, and that could cause the encounter to deteriorate into an adversarial confrontation that would make it far more difficult to get Ronald to confess to the theft.

Rather than sit in judgment, Phil launched into his monologue:

"Ronald, first of all, let's get some things straight here—let's make sure we're on the same sheet of music. What we're talking about here is forty dollars. We're not talking about someone meticulously planning a bank robbery. This is a situation where, I promise you, there are a couple of things going on with the person who did this. This person did this on the spur of the moment. And that begs the question of why he felt he had to do it. It's probably because he's under some kind of pressure that most other people don't know about."

No resistance. "What do you mean?" Ronald asked. His calm voice evincing compassion, Phil pressed on:

"Ronald, look. Money is one of those things in life that we panic over. We need to look at this from that perspective. Think of your kids: If the phone rang and the person on the other end told you that one of your kids was in a car accident, there's an element of panic—you're not really thinking clearly. All you know is that you have to drop whatever you're doing, no matter how important it is, and get to your kid. At that moment, that's all you care about. It's the same thing with money. There are some times when people do something they wish they hadn't done—they just do it on the spur of the moment, because they're not thinking clearly. What's really important here, Ronald, are two things: Whether you're sorry, and whether you're willing to give it back. If we can cover those two bases, we can go a long way toward resolving this issue. As I'm sitting here, Ronald, you look like you're feeling pretty bad."

Ronald took a deep breath, and exhaled. "Yeah," he said.

"Are you sorry?" Phil asked gently.

"Yeah, I am," Ronald said. He pulled out his wallet, took out the two twenty-dollar bills, and handed them to Phil. The entire process had taken less than ten minutes. Yet if Phil had allowed the seriousness of the situation to stir his emotions, he might never have gotten to that point. Ronald likely would have become equally emotional, and the engagement might have degenerated into an acrimonious standoff.

Ronald, a good guy who did a stupid thing, ultimately kept his job. He received a reprimand and a memorandum for the record in his security file, but his career wasn't ruined. Phil's unemotional, nonjudgmental approach helped Ronald to man up—to admit his mistake, and to demonstrate remorse. Because of that, Ronald got a second chance.

In order to avoid doing harm, it's helpful to understand the psychological dynamics at play in the interrogator's quest to get the truth. Think of the interrogation as a stage with two actors whose roles have opposing agendas. The first actor did the bad thing, and his role in the production is to convince the second actor, the interrogator, that he didn't do the bad thing. To accomplish his goal, the first actor must lie and deny, because he fears the consequences that could ensue from his bad behavior. He perceives the interrogator as the enemy— someone who is out to get him, someone who could cost him his job or his family, someone who could cause him embarrassment and shame, or even send him to jail. In essence, the interrogator is someone who could ruin his life.

This scenario describes the traditional view of an interrogation. It is, by its very nature, confrontational and adversarial. But this "me against you" approach is clearly counterproductive, and a nonstarter for a successful interrogation.

The far better approach is for the interrogator to distance himself from the decision makers who will determine the consequences of the confession. For that to happen, it's essential for the interrogator to be perceived as a mediator or a negotiator—a middleman between the subject and a higher authority, whether that authority is the criminal justice system, the board of directors, the administration, upper management, the union, the teacher, or even a parent. On the interrogation stage, in other words, the actor playing the interrogator projects the image that his purpose is to accompany the actor playing the bad guy to help him navigate his way to a solution of his problem. The interrogator will begin to be seen as a confidant— someone who can be relied upon to help achieve an equitable outcome. Consequently, any hostile feelings that initially may have been projected onto the interrogator will likely subside.

Michael was once called in to help a small police department resolve a heinous felony child abuse case that provided an enlightening example of the power and effectiveness of this mediator approach. A young man we'll call "Tommy" reported that he had discovered his live-in girlfriend's eight-month-old daughter, whom we'll call "Belinda," had obvious head trauma, including bruising and extensive swelling. When the paramedics arrived, they found Belinda pale and unresponsive, with labored breathing and a faint pulse.

Michael interviewed Belinda's mother, who said she had been at the welfare office when the baby suffered the injuries, and concluded that she had been truthful. The investigation therefore turned to Tommy, who claimed he had no idea how the child's injuries had been sustained. Michael interviewed Tommy, and observed a large number of deceptive behaviors, so he switched into interrogation mode. Michael was proceeding with the interrogation when, to his surprise, the detective with whom he had been working on the case suddenly came into the interrogation room. He had decided that Michael wasn't making any headway, and came in to release Tommy to give him a chance to "think it over."

Michael was stunned. He had Tommy squarely in short-term thinking mode, and sensed he was on the verge of a confession. He knew that once Tommy left to do all of that pondering, the short-term thinking would collapse, and the chance of getting the truth would likely be lost forever. The detective handed Tommy his business card, and asked him to call him on Monday after he had thought it over. Tommy got up from his chair, and as he approached the door to leave, Michael knew he had to do something, and quickly. That baby girl needed justice, and he wasn't about to let his best chance of accomplishing that slip through his fingers.

"Tommy, why can't you tell us now?" Michael asked, managing to maintain his calm bearing.

"Because I'm scared, Michael," Tommy replied. "I'm scared."

In the world of interrogation that was tantamount to a confession, and it was all Michael needed to hear.

"I understand that, Tommy," Michael said. "But you sincerely need to rethink this. If you leave now, it will be out of my hands for good. I'm here to work with you, and you need to clear it up. You need to clear it up today. You need to clear it up now. You owe it to yourself, and most importantly, you owe it to little Belinda."

Tommy sat back down. After several more minutes of talking with Michael and the detective, Tommy was in tears. He turned to Michael.

"You're pretty smart," Tommy said. "What would you do?"

Michael looked at Tommy the way a father would look at a son who had come to him for advice. "I would tell the truth," he replied gently. "That's what I would do."

Tommy looked down, and slowly nodded. He proceeded to give a full confession.

Tommy saw Michael as an ally, someone who wanted to help him deal with this nightmare he was living. That persuaded Tommy to share the truth: On the third day of a methamphetamine binge, he inflicted the injuries on the baby girl because her crying was keeping him awake.

Over the course of a long career, Michael had encountered the worst of the worst—murderers, rapists, child abusers—so he had been there plenty of times with people like Tommy. But what shouldn't be lost in all of this is that Michael genuinely cared about Tommy. In fact, everything he told Tommy was from the heart—he understood what Tommy was feeling. Tommy knew that, and he ultimately turned to Michael for advice in making what would be one of the most important decisions of his life.

As Tommy was being handcuffed and escorted from the interrogation room, he turned to Michael.

"I bet you hate me, don't you," he said, the pain of the thought evident in his voice.

"Tommy, I hate what you did," Michael replied, with no need to fake the compassion that Tommy could clearly see. "But I don't hate you."

# AN ELICITATION CASE STUDY
||||||||||||||||||||||||||||||||||||||||||||||||||||||||||

A sixteen-year-old girl we'll call "Judy" let something slip in a casual conversation with the female dispatcher at a local police department. Judy, who worked at the station as a member of the Police Explorers, an auxiliary police program for young people, mentioned to the dispatcher that she had engaged in a sex act with an officer on the force. What Judy didn't realize at the time was that the police officer, whom we'll call "Ralph," was dating the dispatcher.

The dispatcher, as you might imagine, was furious, and she reported the incident to the police chief. Ralph, a handsome twenty-four-year-old who was well liked by everyone in the department, vehemently denied the accusation, which had to do with an incident of mutual masturbation in Ralph's truck. Following an internal investigation, everyone involved—the police chief, lieutenants, sergeants, the investigator from the district attorney's office—believed that Ralph was telling the truth, and that Judy had fabricated the entire story. Even Judy's father was overheard screaming at her, "I want you to stop fucking lying to these men, and tell them the truth!"

Judy's physical description of Ralph's genitals was inaccurate (we'll spare you the details), and there were apparent inconsistencies in her story as to where the act took place. But what really convinced the investigators that she was lying was her "lack of emotion" in recounting the details of the incident. They were certain that a sixteen-year-old girl's behavior would be akin to that of a traumatized rape victim if she had been telling the truth, so her composure in recounting the incident was seen as a conspicuous red flag. But Judy stuck unwaveringly to her story.

That's when Michael entered the scene. He was called in to interview Judy, and to confirm that she was lying.

It made for a long day. It was a four-hour drive to the town where the police department was located, and Michael was scheduled for an early morning interview with Judy. As the interview got under way, Michael soon recognized that there was a very reasonable explanation for why she had been so composed in recounting the story: She was an enthusiastic participant, and actually had hoped for such an encounter with Ralph. She was anything but traumatized.

Throughout the interview, Michael closely observed the verbal and nonverbal behaviors Judy exhibited in response to his questions, and he came to his conclusion with a high degree of certainty: Judy was telling the truth. That meant Michael needed to have a chat with Ralph.

At the conclusion of the interview with Judy, Michael met with the police chief in his office, along with several of the investigating officers. They were stunned when Michael told them that in his professional opinion Judy was telling the truth. But the police chief didn't hesitate. Ralph was at home, having been placed on administrative leave with pay to wait out the investigation. The police chief called him and ordered him to report immediately to the station for an interview with Michael.

As we pointed out in Chapter 6, it's essential for an interviewer to be as informed as possible about the interviewee's background, so that this information can be incorporated into the monologue, should the interview transition to an interrogation. Michael knew that Ralph had been honorably discharged from the U.S. Marine Corps, and that he was divorced, with a reputation as a ladies' man in the community.

We've found that the more we know about the person's less fortunate life circumstances, the better equipped we will be to develop an effective interrogation strategy. These circumstances might include financial difficulties, alcohol or drug dependency, relationship problems, being raised in a one-parent household or on the wrong side of the tracks, physical abuse, racism, sexism, employment issues, or simple bad luck. All of these circumstances are fertile ground for exploitation as we build rationalization into the monologue.

During the nonaccusatory investigative interview, the interviewer should take advantage of any opportunities that present themselves to begin planting seeds in the event of a subsequent interrogation. In Michael's interview with Ralph, such an opportunity arose when he learned that Ralph's alleged misconduct had been characterized by the investigators in extremely harsh language. This is how it played out:

**Michael:** How did you learn of the allegations against you?

**Ralph:** I was getting ready for work, and they told me to come meet the chief. I was thinking, there are only two reasons for meeting the chief—when you're doing good, or you're doing bad. So I just came in, and they sat me down and the chief told me what the allegations are— that I molested Judy. I didn't know what to think. That's how I heard of it.

**Michael:** That's what he called it—"molesting"? That's the word he used?

**Ralph:** Yeah.

**Michael:** Okay. That's kind of a strong word.

**Ralph:** Yeah.

**Michael:** How did you feel when he said that?

**Ralph:** Like my life had stopped. Those are serious allegations. I couldn't think. I didn't know what to say.

[Michael was thinking, *Hey, Ralph, how about saying, I DIDN'T DO IT!*]

**Michael:** What did you say?

**Ralph:** I didn't say anything. They just walked me out and I sat down and spoke with the Department of Justice investigator.

From that brief exchange, Michael knew that a major psychological hurdle he would need to overcome during the interrogation would require him to reframe the allegation so that it wasn't presented in terms of Judy having been "molested." He needed to use a softer, more psychologically acceptable term, like "inappropriate touching."

Another means of gaining insight into potential psychological hurdles that will need to be overcome during an interrogation is to simply ask. A hypothetical question can be particularly effective, as Michael demonstrated in this case:

**Michael:** If someone did what Judy said happened here, what do you think the person would be afraid of? What would be the person's biggest reason not to want to tell the truth about that? What would be their greatest fear?

**Ralph:** Like if I did it?

**Michael:** You or anybody who had done something like what Judy said happened.

**Ralph:** I guess if they're an adult and she's a minor, I guess worried about going to jail or something.

Bingo! That new information would be solid gold in an interrogation. Now Michael knew the biggest psychological hurdle he'd need to overcome in order to turn Ralph's "no" into "yes" was his fear of going to the Big House should he confess.

Michael had gotten enough information to be convinced that Ralph was indeed lying, so it was time to switch to interrogation mode. His transition statement took the form of a DOG, and he began by explaining how he knew that Ralph wasn't being truthful:

**Michael:** Basically, what we are able to do now is just based upon the way a person looks, acts, and talks, we know whether he is telling the truth or not. Because people do certain things and they say things certain ways when they tell the truth, and they do certain things and say certain things when they don't tell the truth. And, quite frankly here, Ralph, based on the verbal and nonverbal behaviors you have displayed during our interview, and based upon the investigation itself, there is no question that there was sexual activity between you and Judy.

**Ralph:** [Silence]

It's important to note here that throughout the interrogation, you need to remain firmly in what we call "L-squared mode." That is, you need to simultaneously *look* and *listen* to track the subject's verbal and nonverbal behaviors. Beyond the obvious advantage of determining truth and deception, this assessment model serves as a road map to track progress, or lack thereof, as the interrogation unfolds. In this case, Ralph's failure to deny reinforced Michael's initial assessment that Ralph was being deceptive, and that he was on the right course.

Michael threw Ralph a lifeline of hope, sliding into his monologue since Ralph had yet to offer any resistance.

**Michael:** Now, the good news is the verbal and nonverbal behavior you've displayed has shown me that you are not what I would classify as a typical sex offender. You're not even close to that. So, I'm going to be able to say conclusively that you're not necessarily a threat to anybody.

I think when you get down to the brass tacks of this thing, my gut feeling is they are going to find out that this was probably all Judy's idea, and that you absolutely didn't do anything to encourage it, nor did you force anything, and that one thing led to another. We all make mistakes in judgment. But because you are in the law enforcement setting, nobody wants to spoil anything for you. I can tell just from talking to you that you are an outstanding police officer.

I don't want to ruin anything for you. But what's happened here, what I wanted to say, is they should have known better. Through no fault of yours, they have kind of unconsciously put the fear of God in you, and forced you into a position where it's been really hard for you to tell the truth. Had they not labeled it "molestation," I think you would have leveled with them. Had they handled you differently, I think you would have said, "Yeah, it was stupid and I shouldn't have done it." But then they started throwing out those buzzwords that would have scared *me* off. And, because you're new in the profession and you're green, you don't know how these administrative things go. You're fearful of how you may be looked upon. Everybody that I've talked to speaks very highly of you, and that's not going to change based on a silly little thing like this.

Now, if you had forced Judy, if you had got her drunk or gave her drugs or taken advantage of her like that—see, that would have been a whole different thing. But none of that happened. If Judy was eight years old or nine years old, that would be a completely different thing. But she's almost eighteen. She's for all practical purposes an adult. And, twenty-four isn't that old. You're not that much beyond her age.

Ralph was nodding in agreement.

**Michael:** Now, if I was with Judy—I'm fifty-one years old—then people might look at that and say that's weird, that's age inappropriate. I'm not real quick with math, but I know fifty-one minus sixteen—that's a lot of years, and so that would be really embarrassing for me. Or if Chief here ended up with Judy, that would be really embarrassing.

I'm married. I don't know if Chief is married. He probably is, but you're not even married, see, so, these kinds of things happen in the workplace all the time. There's always sexual tension in the workplace. And I'm not even implying that you had the hots for Judy, because I know you didn't. I'm not implying that you singled her out or selected her and then seduced her, went after her. That's not the case at all.

All that's happened here is, my gut is, she came to you, saw you as someone she was attracted to and said, "Hey, Ralph, can you give me a ride home?" And you thought it was an innocent thing. And, you're a nice guy, thinking nothing's behind it. Why not give her a ride home? And then one thing led to another, and then this thing happened and you think it's no big deal, just a quickie, a one-night-stand kind of thing, and not that much happened anyway. And for all you knew, it was over with, and no big deal. And then months later they come to you. You had probably completely forgotten about it, and then all of a sudden here it is, and it's taken on a life of its own. And it's silly. It's unfortunate.

They don't want to be wasting their time on something goofy like this, because it's just goofy. They want to resolve it so everyone can move on. And you can move on and do what you've got to do because you've got big things ahead of you. You've got an honorable discharge from the Marine Corps. You're on track. Everything career-wise is on track, and my guess is you'll probably get some education along the way somewhere, too. You've got big plans, and there's no reason that can't continue.

But part of being in law enforcement is being honest. And it's hard to be honest sometimes not knowing for sure what's going to happen or knowing how people are going to view you. But one thing you should know is we all blow things out of proportion. Anything we do wrong, we magnify it because we're talking about ourselves. It makes us feel guilty, and we're ashamed.

It's the good people that magnify things, the good people that are hard on themselves. And you've been at this game long enough to know that it's the bad people that don't care, it's the bad people who think what they did isn't that big of a deal, even robbing and raping and killing. In their world it's just another day at the beach. It's just part of their whole lifestyle. In your world and in my world, even speeding makes us feel guilty. This particular thing probably didn't make you feel guilty when it happened because it was consensual and she agreed to do it, she enjoyed it. You didn't force her to do anything, and then you took her home. She actually bragged to her friends because she was proud of it, and it was no big deal.

It's when it accidentally leaked out that they felt compelled to follow up on it a little bit so that they could kind of nip this thing in the bud to make sure that, first of all, you're not the kind of person who would force someone. Second of all, that you're not the kind of person that would try to do this with someone who was five or six years old. That's what I call molestation.

Getting back to what I said, when you work in law enforcement, gosh darn it, you have to bite the bullet sometimes because we all make mistakes. Everybody who works here or any other police department, they've all done some things that they have regretted; done some things they knew they shouldn't have done. But we're all human. Don't let this ruin your career. One little mistake. People make mistakes all the time.

**Ralph:** If I say it happened, my career in law enforcement is over.

That was a very informative comment from Ralph. His continued lack of denial was strengthening Michael's belief that Ralph did, in fact, molest Judy. And he was expressing his reason for resisting the idea of confessing.

**Michael:** Who knows?
**Ralph:** I know.
**Michael:** How do you know that?
**Ralph:** I just know.
**Michael:** We'll deal with that, but first of all we need to

get something going for you. I mean if I just walk out of here and say, "Hey, Ralph did it and he just doesn't care. He doesn't even care enough to tell the truth . . ."
**Ralph:** I care.
**Michael:** I know you care, and I want you to care. It's obvious that you care. I want to be able to show that you worked with me. I want to be able to show that you cooperated. I want to be able to show that you are sorry. I want to be able to show that you are never ever going to do anything like this again because I truly, honestly believe that. I need to tell them that you resolved it.

At that point, Ralph had his face in his hands, and he was beginning to cry.

**Michael:** You're not a molester. For them to say that is not accurate, and I'm going to tell them that because I know you're not. I know you're not, Ralph.

Michael sensed that Ralph might have been psychologically prepared to tell the truth, so he decided it was time to evaluate his progress by asking a presumptive question.

**Michael:** Was it her idea?
**Ralph:** No, it wasn't my idea. Nothing was my idea.

Ralph apparently misheard the question, perhaps because he was expecting Michael to ask if it was his idea.

**Michael:** Was it her idea?
**Ralph:** I was taking her home.
**Michael:** I know that. It's over, Ralph. You've got to tell the truth. This is hard. I know it's hard. I know you're strong. I know you've got the courage to do it. But the

last thing you need is to walk away from it without clearing it up, because then people are going to think the worst about you. There is no reason for anybody to do that. We're going to handle this discreetly. I'm just going to talk to the investigators about it, but we need to clear it up.

**Ralph:** What's going to happen?

Ralph's statement was one of resignation. It was a critical turning point in the interrogation. He was no longer resisting, but rather weighing his options to determine whether confessing was or was not his best course of action, depending upon the punishment that would lie ahead. It is at this point that some interrogators succumb to the temptation to make threats, or to make promises they can't keep. Falling into this trap will invalidate the confession in any court of law. It's essential that you never make threats or promises in an interrogation scenario. If there's a Golden Rule in elicitation, it is this: Never do or say anything that could make an innocent person confess.

**Michael:** I'm glad you brought that up. First, I don't know the answer to that. What I do know is there are a variety of means of resolving these matters, and prosecution is only one of them. This is a very important decision that will affect your future, your career as a law enforcement officer. The people that make the decision are going to have to consider some things, and this is what they'll have to consider. They'll have to decide whether you have been completely truthful and cooperative, whether you're honest. Second, they will want to know if you genuinely understand that you made a mistake, and that you care enough to clear it up. I want to be able to tell them that Ralph cares. They'll want to know that you had the guts to admit your mistake, and that you will never make this same mistake again. I want to be able to tell them that, and it's important. Most importantly, they'll want to know that you are sorry for what you did. And I want to be able to tell them that he's sorry, he's really sorry. I want to be able to tell them that there was no force, and that it was consensual. It was a one-time thing, spur-of-the-moment. Something you didn't plan out. It just happened, and it was absolutely out of character for you. I want to be able to tell them that. So whoever makes the decision about your future, those are the important things they'll want to have answers to. And, unless you clear it up, you're going to make their decision easy, very easy. But if you own up to it and you apologize, and you say you're sorry, and you care and they see that, and they already like you, and they already think the world of you, then these people are going to come to what I would say is a very reasonable decision that you all can live with. But the first step is to break through that denial that you're in right now. That's the first step. And that's the part that would bother them. I know you're sorry, I know you're sorry. I know you feel bad.

Michael, again sensing that Ralph might be ready to confess, decided to once again evaluate his progress by asking another presumptive question.

**Michael:** Is Judy the only one this ever happened with?

Ralph was crying. He nodded his head in a "yes" motion. That was the truth that Michael had been working to elicit. And that's a critical distinction: The goal of any ethical interrogator is never to get a confession, but rather to get the truth.

In this case, the truth was indeed a confession, and Michael needed to corroborate it. That effort often involves handling a great deal of emotion and further resistance.

> **Michael:** That's what I thought.
> **Ralph:** [Crying]
> **Michael:** It's all right. It's all right. I know it's tough. After it happened, did you feel guilty, or did you just kind of think, well, this will go away?
> **Ralph:** [Crying, not responding]
> **Michael:** Tell me what led up to it. How it all happened.
> **Ralph:** I don't remember.

In an interrogation situation, guilty suspects frequently exhibit selective memory. In this case, it took the form of resistance in an attempt to avoid providing incriminating information. It can be frustrating, but it's essential that you not allow it to make you confrontational. Michael took it in stride.

> **Michael:** Well, you remember enough.
> **Ralph:** She just said, "Take me home."
> **Michael:** All right. And then what happened?
> **Ralph:** I don't know. We just drove. I don't even know where we were at.
> **Michael:** Okay.
> **Ralph:** [Continues to cry]
> **Michael:** It's all right, it's all right. It's tough.
> **Ralph:** I've ruined my whole life.
> **Michael:** Oh, no, no, no. Not even close. It seems like that now. It really does. It seems like that now, but it doesn't have to, not at all, not at all. And like I said before, don't blow this out of proportion. This is not that big of a deal.
> **Ralph:** Yeah, it is.

**Michael:** Well to you, I know, to you. I know to you at this point in time it is. It's a big deal to you. But you didn't kill anybody. You didn't rape anybody. You didn't hurt anybody.

**Ralph:** Yeah, but I'm going to jail.

**Michael:** Well, what did the DA investigator tell you they were going to do?

**Ralph:** I don't know. He was hitting me hard.

**Michael:** Well, I don't know. Who am I to know whether you are going to jail or not? Let me ask you this: Did you have sexual intercourse with her?

**Ralph:** Oh, God no!

**Michael:** Why did you guys stop?

**Ralph:** I don't know. I don't even remember. I don't even remember. I don't even remember why we stopped. No clue. I just remember we stopped. I just said, "Let's go."

**Michael:** Were you starting to feel a little weirded out about what was going on? You started to realize what you were doing was wrong and felt kind of bad about it?

**Ralph:** [Crying, nodding his head in a "yes" motion]

**Michael:** See, that's good. That's good. If you were a bad person, you wouldn't have thought there was anything wrong with it.

**Ralph:** I can't look the people in the face.

**Michael:** It's all right, all right. Tell me about what happened that night in the truck.

**Ralph:** [Crying] All I remember is that . . . oh, man.

**Michael:** Come on, Ralph.

**Ralph:** I don't know. I was just thinking how . . . oh, God . . . you know, her touching me and me touching her and then I stopped.

**Michael:** The only thing that touched your penis was her hand?

**Ralph:** Uh-huh.

**Michael:** Okay. About how long did that last while she was masturbating you?

**Ralph:** Seconds.

**Michael:** What would you guess?

**Ralph:** Ten seconds maybe, I don't know. I don't even like that.

People who confess almost always minimize their conduct, so getting the full story can be like squeezing blood from a turnip. Indeed, rarely do we ever get the complete story. The goal is to get as close to the full truth as possible, so the decision makers have as much accurate information as possible upon which to administer justice. Also noteworthy here is Ralph's classic convincing statement, "I don't even like that." Deceptive indicators frequently appear throughout interrogations, and help to serve as a map to where to dig more deeply for additional information.

**Michael:** Tell me about putting your finger into her vagina.

**Ralph:** I just like rubbed . . . fuck.

**Michael:** At least the tip of your finger went in her vagina a little bit, right?

**Ralph:** [Crying, nodding his head in a "yes" motion]

**Michael:** How long would you say your finger was in her vagina?

**Ralph:** Not even a minute—thirty seconds. This whole thing maybe lasted enough to pull over, five seconds; not five seconds, but a short time. I can't live with this.

**Michael:** Yes, you can. You will, you will. It's hard now. It's hard now, but it will pass, it will pass.

**Ralph:** I'm done, I'm done.

**Michael:** We don't know that. We don't know that.

Often at this point in an interrogation, guilty suspects who have confessed perceive their whole world to be crashing down upon them. Consequently, they must be handled delicately, and with a great deal of understanding and compassion. They must be restored psychologically, so they can depart with as much respect and dignity as possible. We've found it's very helpful in that situation to remember the adage "There, but for the grace of God, go I."

**Ralph:** I loved it here, too. Sorry. I just don't know what to think right now. My girlfriend's going to leave me.

**Michael:** We don't know that. How long have you been with her?

**Ralph:** Not long. A few months.

**Michael:** She cares about you.

**Ralph:** Yeah, but . . .

**Michael:** She might not even have to find out about this. Let's wait and see where this thing's going to go. All right?

**Ralph:** I've got to tell all my lieutenants that I lied to them.

**Michael:** No, no. They've all been lied to before. I'm sure they've lied to other people themselves. You're a human being. That's all you are. That's all I am.

**Ralph:** They trust me and I betrayed their trust. And this ain't cheap! [Ralph was referring to the fee for Michael's professional services.]

**Michael:** [Laughs] This is tax dollars, this is tax dollars. This is nothing. Don't worry about that. This is the least of your worries. People are going to respect you. People are going to respect you—that you had the guts to own up to it.

**Ralph:** Yeah, but I should have told them.

**Michael:** Look, and I wasn't kidding before when I told

you, if they'd handled you differently, if they hadn't scared you away in the beginning, I think you would have told the truth. I really do. Don't you think?

**Ralph:** Yeah, when they told me I molested her . . .

**Michael:** I know that. I know that.

At that point, the lieutenant overseeing the investigation was brought into the interrogation room. Ralph repeated his confession in the lieutenant's presence. In the end, he didn't go to jail. He was terminated, but he was later hired by another police department. And Judy was vindicated.

# 12.

# IF O. J. SIMPSON DID IT: THE INTERROGATION THAT MIGHT HAVE BEEN

IIIIIIIIIIIIIIIIIIIIIIIIIIIIIIIIIIIIIIIIIII

On the evening of June 12, 1994, Nicole Brown Simpson and her friend, Ron Goldman, were savagely murdered at Nicole's home in Brentwood, California. On October 3, 1995, Nicole's ex-husband, Orenthal James Simpson—the football hero turned movie star who had been charged with the murders—was acquitted in what many see as one of the most egregious miscarriages of justice in U.S. history.

In late 2006, a publisher announced the pending release of a book by Simpson, titled *If I Did It*, a hypothetical account of a scenario in which Simpson committed the murders. Public outrage in response to the announcement compelled the publisher to cancel the release. Ultimately, a Florida bankruptcy court awarded the book rights to the Goldman family, which in January 2008 published *If I Did It: Confessions of the Killer*. The book includes Simpson's original manuscript, and provides an invaluable psychological insight into the mind of the hypothetical killer.

The assignment to question Simpson when he was brought in by the Los Angeles Police Department the day after the murders fell to LAPD detectives Philip Vannatter and Thomas Lange. The encounter commenced at 1:35 in the afternoon, and was terminated just thirty-two minutes later. It took the form of an interview—Vannatter and Lange never interrogated Simpson.

Our review of the transcript of that interview, the full text of which can be found in Appendix III, has prompted us to consider a hypothetical situation of our own: What would have happened if we had questioned Simpson that day?

Before we proceed any further, it's essential to make clear the fact that our aim is not to disparage Vannatter, Lange, or the LAPD in any way. We have the utmost respect for the men and women of the LAPD—in fact, we have had opportunities to conduct training for the department in the past, and we have highly valued those engagements. Beyond that, we are very much aware that there's nothing particularly valiant or laudable about the role of Monday morning quarterback, especially when it's performed with the benefit of nearly two decades of hindsight. It's just a matter of the Simpson case having gained such widespread notoriety, and the fact that so many people are familiar with it to one degree or another even after all these years, that lends the case so compellingly to examination here. Our purpose, then, is not to claim that our hypothetical encounter with Simpson would necessarily have been fruitful, since any such claim is obviously impossible to substantiate. It is imperative that readers be very clear that the responses we have attributed to Simpson in this exercise are purely hypothetical. They reflect our speculation, based on years of experience in other elicitation scenarios, of what Simpson might have said had he been questioned using the methods described in this book. The exercise is intended to illustrate, as coherently as possible, how the interview and elicitation process is meant to be executed from beginning to end.

With that understood, let's go back to that June day in 1994, and imagine that we're the ones who got the call to question Simpson. Our approach would have recognized that in a law enforcement situation, such an encounter begins with an objective interview. Whether or not the interview transitions to an interrogation would depend on the case facts, the evidence that had been collected to that point, and the information gleaned from the interview. For the purpose of this exercise, we'll put Michael in the questioner's seat. What follows is the approach we would have taken, and what we see as the way it might have unfolded, based on the experience we've had in such cases.

**Michael:** O.J., please come in and have a seat. My name is Michael Floyd, and I will be asking you some questions this afternoon about the deaths of your ex-wife, Nicole, and a young man who we have now identified as Ronald Goldman. Do you mind if I call you "O.J."?

**Simpson:** No, that's what most people have called me my entire life. I'm fine with that.

**Michael:** O.J., before we get into it, I need to take care of some preliminary housekeeping tasks, if you don't mind. First, may I see some identification, please?

**Simpson:** [Produces his California driver's license]

[Michael records the information and notices that Simpson is favoring a bandaged middle finger on his left hand.]

**Michael:** The final thing I need to do before we get started is to read you your constitutional rights per our conversation with your attorney, Howard Weitzman. Are you okay with that?

**Simpson:** Yes. I've got nothing to hide.

**Michael:** I'm glad to hear you say that. O.J., you have the right to remain silent. If you give up the right to remain silent, anything you say can and will be used against you in a court of law. You have the right to speak to an attorney and to have an attorney present during the questioning. If you so desire and cannot afford one, an attorney will be appointed for you without charge before questioning. Do you understand your rights?

**Simpson:** Yeah.

**Michael:** Do you have any questions about that?

**Simpson:** No.

**Michael:** Do you wish to give up your right to remain silent and talk with me today?

**Simpson:** Uh, yes.

**Michael:** Do you give up your right to have an attorney present while we talk?

**Simpson:** Yeah.

**Michael:** First of all, O.J., thank you very much for coming in. We appreciate your willingness to do that. We know you're very concerned about your children, and that you're eager to get back to them to make sure they're okay. So while there is a lot to cover, we're going to stick to the most important issues. O.J., I think the most important thing we need to ask you about is, what happened at Nicole's last night?

**Simpson:** [Behavioral pause] What happened at Nicole's last night? You're asking me what happened at Nicole's last night? How would I know what happened? I was in Chicago. I wasn't anywhere near there last night.

**Michael:** I understand. Let me explain to you that, obviously, this is a very important case because of who you are. I know you would want us to have every available officer working on this case, and I can assure you we do—every resource we can muster is being tapped to resolve it. As a matter of fact, as we speak, we have officers scouring Nicole's neighborhood and your neighborhood, trying to figure this thing out, and we've been developing some interesting information. O.J., is there any reason that any of the neighbors will tell us they saw you in Nicole's neighborhood last night?

**Simpson:** [Behavioral pause] Well, um . . . um . . . I do occasionally pass through the neighborhood, and sometimes I stop to check on the kids. It's only ten minutes from my house, and now that I think about it, I did drive through last night, but I didn't see any lights on, so I didn't stop.

**Michael:** Thanks for that. That's helpful to know. I have to ask you, O.J., was it you who caused the deaths of Nicole and that young man last night?

**Simpson:** Are you kidding me? I loved Nicole with all of my heart. She's the mother of my kids. I didn't even know the other guy. This is crazy, man, really crazy. Do you think I killed them?

**Michael:** That's why we're having this conversation right now, so you can help us sort this thing out. My only objective is to find out what happened, so everyone involved can begin to put their lives back together. Before I get into some specific questions, I'd like you to walk me through your activities last night, starting at nine P.M. and ending at eleven P.M. Please be as absolutely detailed as you can be, okay?

**Simpson:** Okay. Let's see, I went to Sydney's dance recital at Paul Revere High School. It ended about six-thirty, quarter to seven, something like that, you know, in the ballpark, right in that area. Nicole was there with her family, her mother and father, sister, my kids, you know. I remember Nicole was wearing a short skirt that would have looked inappropriate on a sixteen-year-old. She looked ridiculous. Her mother said something about me joining them for dinner but I said no thanks. I went home for a while and dumped my Bentley and got my Bronco. I went looking for my girlfriend, Paula, for a while but she wasn't home. I was calling her and she wasn't around, so I went back to the house. It must have been eight-something, maybe. Kato was there. He hadn't done a Jacuzzi . . . we had . . . we went and got a burger, and I'd come home and kind of leisurely got ready to go. I mean, we'd done a few things. That's about it, I guess. I think you know the limo driver picked me up right around eleven.

**Michael:** Thanks for that, O.J. But maybe I didn't make myself clear enough earlier. What I'm most interested in has to do with what you did between the hours of nine P.M. and eleven P.M. last night. You said you got back to your house at maybe eight-something. Let's pick up your activities from there. Why don't you walk me through in detail what you did until the limo driver picked you up, okay?

**Simpson:** Man, everything is a blur right now. It's hard to remember exactly what I did.

**Michael:** I can understand that, O.J., but it's extremely important to nail some things down, so I need you to do the very best you can to reconstruct your activities, all right?

**Simpson:** Let's see, I remember that I leisurely packed for my trip. I chipped some golf balls in the yard. I took a nap and then the limo driver rang the house and woke me up because I had overslept.

**Michael:** Earlier you mentioned having driven by Nicole's house to see if they were home. Tell me about that.

**Simpson:** Oh yeah, sorry about that. I forgot about doing that. Let me think. Maybe after Kato and I got back from McDonald's, I jumped in the Bronco and took a real quick ride over there on the off chance I might catch them. It must have been nine at the latest.

[Michael recognizes the unintended message. Simpson's phrase, "catch them," is likely what motivated him to drive to Nicole's house. The reason may have been to catch Nicole with her lover.]

**Michael:** Describe your trip to Nicole's house in detail: the route you took to and from, who you were with, who you saw, who you talked to, what you did at Nicole's—your best guess on when you left your house and when you returned.

**Simpson:** Wow. Okay. It was just me. I went south on Rockingham, left on Highwood Street, right on Bristol, left on Sunset, right on Bundy. I went home the same way. I always take that route. It's only about six minutes. Like I said, the lights at Nicole's were off, so I figured either the kids were already in bed or they hadn't gotten home yet. So I just kinda went home and that's about it, as far as I remember.

**Michael:** What time did you leave your house on Rockingham?

**Simpson:** About nine-fifteen or so, I think.

**Michael:** Could it have been before nine?

**Simpson:** No.

**Michael:** Could it have been after nine-thirty?

**Simpson:** No way. I'm really sure about that one.

**Michael:** Why is that?

**Simpson:** Because I needed to take a shower and finish packing before my trip.

**Michael:** Who did you see during the trip to and from Nicole's?

**Simpson:** Not a soul. Trust me.

**Michael:** Who did you talk to during the trip to and from Nicole's?

**Simpson:** Not a soul. Trust me.

**Michael:** What did you do while you were at Nicole's?

**Simpson:** Nothing. Like I said, I just drove by.

**Michael:** At any time did your car ever come to a stop at Nicole's?

**Simpson:** I probably slowed down a little, but I'd have to say I didn't stop, man, and that's the honest to God truth.

**Michael:** At any time did you enter her alley?

**Simpson:** That's where I park when I go over there.

**Michael:** Last night between nine and eleven, did you park your Bronco at Nicole's, even for just a short time?

**Simpson:** Not that I remember, no.

**Michael:** O.J., I want you to give this next question some serious thought. Is there any reason that someone would have told us that they saw your white Bronco parked at Nicole's last night?

**Simpson:** Who said they saw me?

**Michael:** I'm not saying at this point anyone saw you, but if someone tells us they did, it's important you clear it up now, because that could explain a lot of things. Just because someone saw you doesn't mean you hurt anybody. It's possible you had a good reason for being there that is completely unrelated to what happened. If that's the case, we need to clear it up now.

**Simpson:** Well, at this point in time I'm going to stick with what I said unless you know something different that can refresh my memory.

**Michael:** What else should I know about your trip to Nicole's last night?

**Simpson:** That's about it, I think.

**Michael:** Let's revisit the rest of your activities between nine and eleven P.M. Besides your trip to Nicole's, you said you did some leisurely packing, chipped golf balls in your backyard, took a nap, and showered. What else did you do?

**Simpson:** That's it, as far as I can remember.

**Michael:** Did you ever leave your Rockingham estate for any reason after nine-thirty last night, except for when you left in the limo around eleven?

**Simpson:** No.

**Michael:** Is it possible you left your house after nine-thirty for Nicole's, and you could be mistaken?

**Simpson:** I'm going to have to say no. Things were crazy last night. Nicole was up to her old tricks at the recital. Her family was acting weird. I was having some problems with Paula. I had my trip to Chicago to get ready for. You know how it is.

**Michael:** Tell me, O.J., how did you get those injuries on your left hand?

**Simpson:** I don't know. The first time, when I was in Chicago and all, but at the house I was just running around. In Chicago I broke a glass. One of you guys had just called me and I was in the bathroom, and I just went bonkers for a little bit. Last night when I was . . . I don't know, getting my junk out of the car. I was in the house throwing hangers and stuff in my suitcase. I was doing my little crazy what I do, I mean, I do it everywhere. Anybody who has ever picked me up says that O.J.'s a whirlwind. He's running, he's grabbing things, and that's what I was doing. Getting junk out of the car.

**Michael:** To be clear, are you telling me you don't know exactly how you got those injuries on your hand that caused you to bleed so much?

**Simpson:** I really don't.

**Michael:** Do you see the scar on my forehead?

**Simpson:** Yeah.

**Michael:** In 1953, I was sledding down a snow-covered street in Plattsmouth, Nebraska, and went head-first into the bumper of a car parked at the bottom of the hill. This little scar on my calf—barbed wire fence, David City, Nebraska, Public Golf Course, 1963. This little scar below my right eye—Rick Warner elbowed me during basketball practice, 1967. This little scar on my right ankle—number seventy-seven, Grand Island, Nebraska, defensive lineman stomped on me with his steel-tipped cleats when the ref wasn't looking, 1968. This little scar on my right thumb—broken beer bottle, 1981, Northern Virginia. I could go on, but I think you get my point. Your hand injuries—and they look pretty nasty—happened less than twenty-four hours ago, and you cannot give me a coherent explanation for how you sustained them.

[At this point, Michael has very little doubt that Simpson committed the murders. The case facts, the evidence that has been gathered, and the large volume of deceptive behaviors exhibited by Simpson during the interview make it clear that it's time to transition to interrogation mode. Though his level of certainty of Simpson's guilt is high, Michael makes sure that his transition statement covers the entire best-case/worst-case continuum.]

**Michael:** O.J., quite frankly, I have some real concerns here. I think it's only fair that I bring you up to speed on the investigation to date. Here is what I know with certainty, and I ask you to indulge me without interruption until you hear me out. I think what I have to say will be of great interest to you. When I'm done, I'll turn the floor over to you, and you can comment. Is that fair? Do I have your commitment on that?

**Simpson:** Yeah.

**Michael:** Great, O.J. I have so much to share with you, I almost don't know where to begin. Let me begin with the blood. There is a bloody trail leading directly from Nicole's to your house, and the blood was found both outside and inside your house. The white Bronco you admit to driving last night is covered in blood, and we know your Bronco is clearly how the blood was transported from Nicole's to your house. The interesting thing will be confirming whose blood is where, and that won't take us long. There are bloody footprints along Nicole's walkway leading to the alley where you park the Bronco. To the left of the footprints are drops of blood. I'd bet my house that it was your blood dripping from your injured left hand as you returned to your Bronco after the struggle. We found a fresh bloody fingerprint on the knob of the gate leading to the alley where your Bronco is typically parked. Again, I'd bet my house that that fingerprint is yours when you opened the gate with your bloody left hand. There was blood everywhere at Bundy. There is no doubt in my mind that because of the mess, both Nicole's and Ron's blood became commingled with yours and will not only be found in your Bronco, but also at your house. One of our detectives found a bloody glove at Nicole's lying on the ground. Interestingly, it is a left-handed glove that would have left the attacker's left hand exposed to injury. A detective also found a dark-colored knit cap, most likely pulled from the head of the attacker during the struggle, just like the left glove was most likely pulled from the hand of the attacker during the struggle.

Hairs were found in the cap, and we will soon know with scientific certainty who those hairs belong to. Kato heard a loud thump on the outside wall behind his bungalow at Rockingham around ten-forty-five last night, and it scared the shit out of him. He thought it was an earthquake at first. He was too afraid to investigate the small walkway behind his bungalow in the dark. You, interestingly, told him before you left not to call your security company or the police. I think I know why you left him with those instructions now. One of our detectives went behind the bungalow to investigate, and guess what he found: The right-handed mate to the left-handed glove found at Nicole's. The glove found on your property is also covered in blood. No doubt, it will be Nicole's and Ron's blood. We even have a witness, a woman driving a Volkswagen, who says she nearly collided with you last night around ten-forty-five when you ran the red light at the intersection of Bundy and San Vicente on your way back to Rockingham. She said your Bronco rode up onto the center median of San Vicente. Another car, a gray Nissan, also stopped to avoid the collision. The woman said you began honking your horn and shouting at her, "Move your damn car! Move it! Move it!" She lives in the neighborhood and recognized you as the driver. She even took down your license plate number. Detectives found dark clothing in your washing machine and a pair of dark socks on the floor of your bedroom, and those are being blood-typed as we speak. We found an empty Swiss Army knife box next to your tub. My hunch is the forensics lab will come back and say there is a match between the Swiss Army knife and the wounds that were inflicted on Nicole and Ron. Your limo driver got to your house twenty minutes early and rang your buzzer, but of course you didn't answer, because you weren't there.

**Simpson:** [Complete silence, staring straight ahead, motionless]

**Michael:** The driver saw you come back to the house and saw your lights come on in the house around ten-fifty. Look, what happened at Nicole's last night is not the O.J. I know, or the world knows.

**Simpson:** If you think I did it, you don't know me at all.

[It so happens that there are several actual connections between Michael's background and Simpson's. Michael chooses to introduce them here.]

**Michael:** I'm glad you said that, O.J., because I do know you a little bit. You sure as hell won't remember this, but in 1977, a good friend of yours, Sam Denoff, arranged for you to crown my sister, Stephanie, Homecoming Queen at her thirty-first birthday party in the Hollywood Hills, up on Queens Road. There were over a hundred people there, and from what she told me, you were a big hit. She later rented Sam's house at Victoria Beach in Laguna Beach, the house right next door to yours. She spent time with your kids, Arnelle and Jason. She always enjoyed her time with them. My good friend, Don Burpee, played pickup basketball with you at USC every week for two years. He said you were always accessible, and that you always acknowledged him by name around campus. I also have a high school buddy from Nebraska, Denny Hoyle, who was one of your business partners in California Way, the racquetball club up in Pasadena. He always had good things to say about you, too. Heck, you even grew up in the same housing projects on Potrero Hill that my wife did, so I know a little bit about what you had to overcome. Her older sister was Ms. Bronze

California, and is just a couple of years younger than you, and my wife's a doctor now. I even think Danny Glover grew up there. I wouldn't be surprised if my mother-in-law knew your mother, Eunice. It's a small, small world, O.J. My point is, I know firsthand the positive impact you've had on people, and that at your core you've always tried to do the right thing by people. What that tells me is that it wasn't your character that caused you to do this—it was the situation you found yourself in. You measure a person not by a singular act, but by the totality of his life. Don't let this singular act define who you are, O.J. Any coward can lie. The real test of a man is whether he's able to stand up and tell the truth in a difficult situation. You're thinking emotionally right now, rather than rationally, and I can understand that. I understand that you're in a very tough spot right now. I think I understand you a little bit, and I'm here to work with you so we can make some sense out of the craziness of last night. I am absolutely positive that I know the *who* and the *what* that happened. Now all I need to understand is the most important thing, and that is the *why* this thing happened. I know there is an explanation that makes sense, and that's what I want to talk to you about now.

**Simpson:** Why would I kill Nicole? She's the mother of my children. I loved Nicole. And that other guy, I didn't even know him. Why would I want to kill him?

**Michael:** I understand, O.J. From what I know about you, this whole thing is as surreal as it gets. I'm not going to get into all of that domestic violence bullshit between you and Nicole over the years, because I really don't care about that. Husbands and wives know what buttons to push, and things get a little nuts with all of us from time to time when emotions run high. I'm sure there were two sides to all of those stories. What I do care about, though, is last night. I'm not buying the theory that this is the classic "If I can't have you, nobody can" situation. I don't think you were pining to win her back. You both knew it was over.

Let's face it, Nicole had a real temper on her. I've been told if something set her off, she tended to come at you with fists and feet flying, and you had to hold her down sometimes until she could get herself under control. I know you tried like hell to make it work. A couple of years ago, when you guys split, I guess she settled into her new place with the kids. It must have been real tough watching her move forward without you, and knowing she was with other guys in front of your children. I heard she had some questionable friends who were into drugs, and she was becoming more moody and erratic. There was the good Nicole, and the bad Nicole, and it looked like the bad Nicole won. I suspect you were beginning to think she was putting your kids at risk. You had your kids to think about. There's no way you could let her take you down, and the kids with her. She was an accident waiting to happen, and you owed it to your kids to take some action.

I think you went over to her place last night to read her the riot act, and to shake her up a little bit. It sounds like she really needed a wake-up call. This shit was eating you up inside, and it had to stop. You had to get this under control for the kids' sake, and to get on with your own life.

The dark clothes you wore, the knit cap, the gloves, the knife—that was all theater. I know you didn't plan on killing anybody, for two reasons. First, you would never have planned to do this where your kids would find their dead mother. You're far too devoted to them to even consider such a scenario. Second, no one leaves this much evidence lying around Brentwood if they had planned the thing out. You are a very smart guy—too smart for the mistakes that were made. All of this leaves me with only one explanation that makes any sense: It was spur-of-the-moment.

When you get to Nicole's, you park near her back gate. You walk up the path and see candles burning inside, and hear soft music. It's obvious to you that she is expecting company for a romantic encounter. You're pissed because she is doing it again in front of your kids, but you can deal with that. Just then Ron Goldman appears on the scene, while at the same time Nicole hears you drive up, and she's at the front door. Nicole doesn't want to see you, because her lover is there, and she lets you have it. You and Nicole get into it, and now Goldman decides to be a hero and come to Nicole's aid, when in your mind she was in no physical danger whatsoever. Before you can count to three, you're being attacked by two people who overreacted and completely misjudged your intentions. To say this is a bad dream is an understatement. At that moment, your survival instincts kick in, and you're now in the heat of the battle—two against one.

O.J., there are lots of reasons why people do what they do. This isn't the movies; there was no script last night, there was no plan. Sometimes people just can't take the pressure anymore. It just builds and builds. For the most part, you were very good to Nicole. But how did she repay you? By embarrassing you in public, humiliating you, taunting you, trying to make you mad, bad-mouthing you to your children. You simply couldn't let her take down your children with her. Even the strongest person finally just snaps. The next thing you know, it's just happened—your worst nightmare. Last night, what you walked into on Bundy was the perfect storm. In hindsight, I don't see how it could have played out any differently. I don't think there is a person in the world who would not understand how this thing played out.

[Simpson is showing very little emotion, but his head and shoulders are now slumped. He recognizes that it's over.]

**Michael:** O.J., when you drove over to see Nicole last night, did you intend to kill her, or were you just there to protect your kids?
**Simpson:** [Unresponsive]
**Michael:** O.J., the nightmare is over. It's time to wake up. Were you there to protect your kids?
**Simpson:** Yeah. Yeah, I was. Oh, God. My life is over. My life is over. Nobody will forgive me. My life is over.
**Michael:** I knew you were raised to acknowledge your mistakes, and to do something about them. I'm glad you had the guts to tell me the truth, O.J. Guts are something you've been blessed with, or you never would have achieved what you have in life. Of course, I wish this had never happened, but as a public figure I think how you handle yourself from this point on could have a very positive impact on people who are looking for someone with strength. We live in a very forgiving society. If I understand, and I do, other people will understand. You've already got a leg up because of the goodwill you've earned over the years.
**Simpson:** What now?
**Michael:** I'd like to hear how this thing went south so

fast at Nicole's last night, O.J. Let's start with what you did with the knife.

[For the next two hours, Michael questions Simpson about every detail regarding the murders, until he's satisfied that he has covered every element of the crime, and that he has obtained all of the truthful information that Simpson is willing to divulge.]

Is that really the way it would have panned out? Clearly, we have no way of knowing. What we do know is that the outcome of the questioning that day set in motion a sequence of events that prolonged the unspeakable anguish endured by the Brown and Goldman families. And O. J. Simpson, the man later found by a civil court to be culpable for the horrific deaths of the families' loved ones, walked free. He was soon back on the golf course, enjoying life.

There's an interesting footnote to all of this. It so happened that Michael met Detective Lange after Simpson was acquitted, and was able to ask him why he and Detective Vannatter ended their interview after just thirty-two minutes. Lange's response was that they were concerned Simpson would invoke his Fifth Amendment rights, and he would clam up. It was a nonsensical response. In essence, by ending the interview, Lange and Vannatter invoked the Fifth for him. The situation called not for ending the interview, but for keeping Simpson in short-term thinking mode, so that he wouldn't focus on the consequences of his actions, and thus feel compelled to invoke the Fifth to protect himself from them. As it was, Simpson sank a PR hole-in-one by facing his accusers without even having his attorney present. He learned more from the LAPD that day than the LAPD learned from him.

## LESSONS WE HAVE LEARNED

- Understand that exhaustive preparation is absolutely essential. Know your case facts inside and out, identify the most important issues to cover, and formulate the key questions to ask. Take note of gaps in information, inconsistencies, and things that don't fit or add up. Prioritize your issues and questions. Cover your most important issues sooner rather than later. That allows you to manage time constraints, and to take advantage of the suspect's anxiety, which will generally be at its peak at the beginning of the session—the subject will be more likely to exhibit deceptive behaviors that you can analyze. You probably will only have one bite at the apple.

- Have a concrete plan and a well-considered strategy. Identify what it is you want to accomplish. Short of a confession, you must establish specific timelines for the subject's activities, and details regarding his alibi, injuries, and any other key issues. In other words, lock him in tight to a story. The rule of thumb is to be excruciatingly methodical. This sends the message that you will leave no stone unturned.

- When using more than one questioner, ensure that you identify roles beforehand. One questioner takes the lead, while the other observes, takes notes, and considers follow-up questions— all without interrupting. When the first questioner is finished, he turns to the second questioner and "passes the baton" by saying, "That's all I have. Do you have anything?" At this point, the roles reverse. The baton passing continues until both questioners are satisfied that the subject has revealed all of the truthful information he intends to disclose. There are advantages to having only one questioner in the room—remember the maxim "People don't confess to crowds." The baton passing helps create the sense of a one-on-one, rather than a two-on-two, encounter.

- Briefly apprise the subject of exactly what the issue is, and why you're talking to him. Cryptic introductions or "hiding the ball" only work in the movies.

- Collect information in chronological order. Otherwise, you'll risk missing key events or confusing the suspect.

- Don't accept information at face value. Continually test information with follow-up questions: "How do you know that to be so?" "Why do you say that?" "On what do you base that information?"

- Never be afraid to say, "I don't understand." Be absolutely sure to clarify anything that doesn't make sense to you.

- Ask open-ended questions to solicit a narrative response as a means of establishing the basis for the discussion, or of probing an issue. When asking open-ended questions, allow the subject to answer without interruption—the more information he provides, the greater the likelihood that he'll make an inconsistent statement or reveal meaningful information. You want to keep the information faucet flowing. Always test the narrative with follow-up questions.

- Ask close-ended questions to gather specific points of data. Example: "What time did you arrive?"

- Use presumptive questions, sparingly, to convey a presumption about something related to the matter under investigation. Use of this type of question helps to encourage disclosure, because it implies that the interviewer has more information than the subject expected.

- Use bait questions, sparingly, to establish a hypothetical situation that can trigger a mind virus in a deceptive person. Bait questions typically begin with the phrase, "Is there any reason that . . . ?" For example, "Is there any reason that we would find your fingerprints on the doorknob?"

- Ask simple, unambiguous, and straightforward questions. Always avoid asking compound questions, leading questions, negative questions, or questions that are confusing or overly broad.

- Always be alert for follow-up opportunities. Remember to ask, "What else?"

- Avoid falling into the trap of a checklist mentality. Effective interviewing is a very dynamic process, and is much more complex than simply asking a prepared list of questions.

- Keep note taking to a minimum during the interview—you'll be less likely to miss important information conveyed by the subject, and any deceptive behaviors he may exhibit. During an interrogation, don't take any notes at all—if the subject is reminded that you're recording everything he says, he'll be less likely to remain in short-term thinking mode.

- Don't waste time on tangential issues. Ask yourself, "Is this really what we want to know?" "Are we asking high-priority questions here?"

- Don't rush your pace between questions. After the subject responds to a question, take a momentary pause that's just south of awkward before you ask your next question. The brief silence gives you time to digest the response, and to determine what your next question should be. In addition, a guilty person may blurt out a nugget of information that you wouldn't have gotten if you had rushed into your next question.

- Maintain a noncoercive, nonadversarial demeanor throughout the process. Always treat the subject with dignity, respect, and compassion.

- Make the person feel good about disclosing information by rewarding him with statements like, "Thanks for sharing that," or "That's helpful, thank you."

- Always incorporate catch-all questions to uncover lies of omission or information that was overlooked: "What else can we talk about that will help us understand your situation?" "What haven't I asked you today that you think I should know about?"

# 13.
# THE ELEPHANT IN THE ROOM
||||||||||||||||||||||||||||||||||||||||||||||||||||||||||||

In his 2011 book, *The Black Banners*, Ali H. Soufan, a former FBI interrogator, recounted in some detail his perspective on the circumstances surrounding the interrogation of Abu Zubaydah, the first high-value detainee in the United States' War on Terror, who was captured in Pakistan in 2002. Soufan argued that he and his FBI colleagues had been successful in obtaining actionable intelligence from Abu Zubaydah by means of noncoercive, rapport-building interrogation techniques. He maintained that a team from the CIA's Counterterrorism Center, or CTC, subsequently came in with the authority to use enhanced interrogation techniques, and that when those harsh methods were used against Abu Zubaydah, he ceased cooperating, and the intelligence dried up.

Soufan wrote that the CTC team included the Agency's chief operational psychologist; an interrogator he called "Ed"; a polygraph examiner he called "Frank"; and a contractor hired by the CIA—a psychologist he called "Boris." The team was later complemented, Soufan wrote, by a contingent of young CIA analysts.

According to Soufan, the CIA group was sharply divided on

the effectiveness of the enhanced interrogation techniques—a division he portrayed with Boris as the leader of the faction that advocated enhanced interrogation, and Frank as the voice for noncoercive techniques, consistent with those that Soufan and his FBI colleagues had been employing.

Not surprisingly, Soufan was sharply critical of Boris. He wrote that Boris readily acknowledged not only that he had never questioned an Islamic terrorist, but that he had never even conducted an interrogation. Soufan recounted how Boris responded to an argument that the enhanced techniques would be completely ineffective against someone who was committed to dying for his cause:

> "This is science," was Boris's response. He seemed shocked to have someone challenging him. Former colleagues of his told me that he always viewed himself as the smartest person in any room and disliked anyone who questioned him. . . . "You'll see," said Boris. "It's human nature to react to these things. You'll soon see how quickly he folds. Human beings always want to make life better for themselves. You'll see." . . . He had a condescending look on his face, as if he couldn't be bothered with speaking to such simpletons.

Soufan went on to write about what happened after Boris's initial techniques failed to yield the results he had promised.

> Other CTC officials and local CIA officers also began to develop doubts, and their original openness to trying Boris's techniques was replaced by growing skepticism. They had limited or no interrogation experience and didn't know anything about Abu Zubaydah, so at first didn't know better. Boris had seemed to know what he was talking about.

But then they saw that Boris's experiments were evolving into a risky situation with possible legal ramifications. They also began to realize that while Boris came across as being full of confidence, in reality he was just experimenting. His experience was limited to the classroom. He'd never been involved in an actual interrogation of a terrorist before.

Still, according to Soufan, the young CIA analysts who joined the team admired Boris, and were receptive to his arguments. He wrote that the rapport-building, noncoercive approach advocated by Frank, the CIA polygraph examiner, was seen by the young analysts as "boring." Frank's approach was to convince Abu Zubaydah that cooperating was not only in his best interest, but was the right thing to do at that moment in time.

Soufan wrote that Boris hated Frank, which he surmised was due to the fact that Frank was an actual interrogator who made it clear, from what he said and how he conducted his interrogation of Abu Zubaydah, that he disagreed with Boris's approach. Soufan recounted what happened when Boris and the young CIA analysts watched the CCTV monitor when Frank was in with Abu Zubaydah:

> Boris often made sarcastic remarks about Frank to the others in the room: "He's boring the hell out of him," he might say, or "You know what Abu Zubaydah is saying right now? He's saying, 'Just shoot me.'" Some of the young analysts would laugh at anything Boris said.

When we read Soufan's account of the interrogation of Abu Zubaydah, we were struck by its clarity as a microcosm of the enhanced interrogation debate. As we noted in the opening pages of this book, we are disinclined to address the question of what interrogation techniques our country should be prepared to employ to protect our national security, or to judge anyone who advocates any particular technique. But what we are prepared to do is to offer our own perspective on what Soufan recounted in his book, with the understanding that we are not in a position to vouch for its accuracy.

To the extent that Soufan's portrayal was at least close to being factual, what's essential to understand is that Boris's contention that it's human nature to immediately provide truthful information as a reaction to physical and mental torment just isn't true. Moreover, it's entirely wrong to suggest that fear is the only driver of influence in an interrogation situation. The fear of being subjected to physical and mental torment is likely to elicit a reaction, but its reliability in eliciting truthful information is suspect, at best.

The efficacy of our approach to getting the truth simply goes far beyond the understanding of people like Boris. That lack of understanding is at least partially attributable to a convoluted notion of how short-term thinking works.

In fact, when the aim is to elicit the truth, short-term thinking isn't about *instilling* fear—it's about *minimizing* or *eliminating* it. In the case of Abu Zubaydah, if we have reason to believe that this man is withholding information about individuals involved in terrorist attacks, our best chance of influencing him to release that information is to get him to a place where he's not thinking about any negative consequences of releasing it. The absence of fear, rather than its presence, is the driver. Boris appeared to be unable to grasp that concept.

The approach that Boris advocated accomplishes a purpose: It produces information from the individual upon whom the physical and mental abuse is being inflicted—the assumption being not only that the individual has the information the abuser is seeking in the first place, but that the information he provides to alleviate his suffering is truthful. Everybody wins—the abuser gets his information, and the individual gets the pain to stop. But what Boris apparently couldn't grasp is that the assumption is entirely unfounded, and that the premise is necessarily a false one. It's also one that raises an essential question: Was a problem solved, or was one created? History will ultimately be the arbiter.

What we as a nation, and as a global community, need to ask ourselves is whether we're prepared to go the route of abuse and torment, and where that route will eventually lead. Beyond the question of whether it will take us to a place where we're able to get the truth, we have to consider the slippery slope down which that route might go. If we decide it's acceptable to take this approach with terrorists, then who's to say it shouldn't be taken with sex offenders, white-collar criminals, or reckless drivers? At what point down the slope does it stop?

The approach we've shared with you in this book is one that has proven throughout our careers to be unmatched in enabling people in all walks of life, and in the broadest of circumstances, to get the truth. But there's more to it than that. It's an approach that is wholly consistent with the moral standards that have been taught through the ages by the world's religious traditions. It's consistent with the legal and ethical principles upon which the United States was founded. And it's consistent with the values that the Central Intelligence Agency has striven to uphold since its inception.

We're happy to stay the course.

# ELABORATION ON APPLYING THE ELICITATION MODEL IN BUSINESS, IN LAW, AND IN EVERYDAY LIFE: CHAPTER COMMENTARY BY PETER ROMARY

||||||||||||||||||||||||||||

## INTRODUCTION

The elicitation methodology that Phil, Michael, and Susan have shared in this book is a remarkably powerful mechanism for getting the truth in an interpersonal encounter. As they've shown, its power lies, to a large extent, in the broad nature of its relevance. The techniques they've developed and practiced in the intelligence and law enforcement arenas have widespread applicability well outside those realms, they've explained, in undertakings as routine as hiring an employee or purchasing a car. The common thread that weaves through the experiences they've shared, from interrogating a spy to getting to the bottom of employee theft in a retail establishment, is the concept of influence. It's a concept that warrants elaboration in this section of the book, as it relates to the everyday situations we all find ourselves in when a desired outcome is dependent on the truthfulness of another party.

As I've tapped the power of influence in my capacity as a negotiator and legal advocate, I've come to recognize that the tools and skills used by the world's top intelligence operatives to vet sources and catch spies are largely the same tools and skills that are used in negotiation situations, whether the aim is to win the release of a hostage, hammer out the terms of a corporate merger, or secure a long overdue pay raise. We stand a far better chance of prevailing in any of these scenarios if we're able to step into the shoes of the other party, so that we can understand where he's coming from—what he knows, what he wants, and what motivates him.

In this part of the book, then, we want to explore the concept of influence that underlies the methodology we've developed to get the truth, and examine how that methodology can be used not only in interviewing and elicitation situations, but in achieving a favorable outcome in any interpersonal exchange in which the two sides have conflicting agendas.

Throughout my career, I have interviewed and elicited information from people under a broad range of circumstances, and I have come to appreciate the role that influence plays in motivating people not only to share truthful information, but to align their agendas more closely with those of the people they're dealing with. I don't pretend for a moment to be the best in my field, but I have learned a great deal along the way, largely from the mistakes I've made and the times I've been beaten. There have been plenty of those. But there is a great deal of consolation in the opportunity to share what I've learned from them.

The following commentaries are intended to help explain what it is that makes our methodology so effective, and to illustrate the crossover between the world of the spy, and the world the rest of us navigate every day.

# Chapter 1

# SPIES, LIARS, AND CROOKS: FOLLOWING THE YELLOW BRICK ROAD

||||||||||||||||||||||||||

What do spies, computer hackers, armed robbers, cheating spouses, and gamblers all have in common? If that sounds like a riddle, it's actually more of a puzzle. All of them, curiously enough, genuinely believe they'll be able to dodge any negative consequences of their actions.

Why did Mary walk into a room and undergo a polygraph examination with one of the most highly skilled interrogators in the world, rather than simply resign from her position with the CIA? Why did Osama bin Laden opt to reside in a conspicuous compound in Abbottabad, Pakistan, less than a mile from a military academy that was visited by U.S. and Allied military personnel? Why do many of us still text and drive? Why do we buy lottery tickets when economists refer to the lottery as an "idiot tax," given that our chances of actually winning the jackpot are typically in the range of a couple of hundred million to one?

The short and simple answer is that these people—indeed, the large majority of us—choose to bask in the eternal sunshine of *optimism bias*.

In L. Frank Baum's novel *The Wonderful Wizard of Oz*,

unlike in the film, upon entering the Emerald City the characters are given green-tinted eyeglasses to wear, so that the city appears to be more green than it really is—we're told in the novel that the city is "no more green than any other city." Think of optimism bias as our tendency to view the world through those glasses, so that what we see is more appealing than the reality of the situation.

Bad stuff, you see, never happens to the biased optimist. Prison time, divorce court, a head-on collision, just aren't in the cards. Before you sit back and think, "What fools," consider this: According to Tali Sharot, a leading researcher in the field, the vast majority of us exhibit optimism bias. For many of us, a small dose of it isn't necessarily a bad thing. But it's important to take stock of any given situation and ensure that we're not risking everything by donning our green-tinted eyeglasses.

Optimism bias occurs when a person believes that an activity he's engaged in carries less risk for himself than it does for another person who engages in the same activity, or that he stands a higher chance of reward. This biased optimism can lead people to engage in risky behavior, because they're convinced they won't be caught, hurt, killed, or victimized by some other negative consequence. Skilled negotiators and interviewers are aware of its existence, recognize it in themselves and others, and adjust their actions accordingly. We know that while we tend to be very optimistic about ourselves, our families, and our friends, we're not as optimistic about the lives of others. So my optimism that I'm going to win my big case is coupled with a belief that the hapless lawyer on the other side is going to have things go horribly wrong for her.

In nearly every nation, it's a crime to lie to law enforcement officials. In some cases, it might be a minor offense called "providing fictitious information to a public officer," with the penalty, at most, probation or a fine. In other circumstances, it may be a case of "perverting the course of justice," which can carry a long prison sentence. Still, people lie to law enforcement officials all the time—in some cases hoping, in many others genuinely believing, they won't be caught.

It's a crime to lie to an immigration officer when entering the United States, just as it is when entering almost any country. Yet consider the case of a man with dual citizenship who was refused a visa to enter the United States on one of his passports because of a criminal conviction in his past. Rather than seek a waiver of exclusion, he used his other passport to enter the country on multiple occasions, risking prosecution not only in the United States, but in the country that issued the passport he used to skirt the law. Clearly, no rational person would do this if he believed he would be caught, as such crimes can carry substantial prison sentences. But with the advanced technology and global data sharing that immigration authorities worldwide now employ, people are prosecuted every day for crimes committed years ago that are just now being discovered. Optimism bias can lead to incredibly risky behavior.

When I think of optimism bias, I'm reminded of a criminal client I represented a number of years ago. My client was accused of stealing a camera and then pawning it. He had told everyone who would listen that he was not guilty—the police, the prosecutor, his family, the jailer; he even told a couple of judges. Finally, his "probable cause" court date arrived, and I was ready to go. The arresting officer, who was a friend of mine—a benefit of having spent years training and representing police officers—asked if we could have a chat out in the hall. Out I went, and the officer produced the camera—a brand-new digital model that, at the time, was quite uncommon. On the camera were several pictures of my client, posing with a smile, that had been taken by the pawnbroker. A problem for my client arose at the shop when he couldn't produce a valid form of identification, so the pawnbroker asked if he could take his picture. My client dutifully obliged, varying his pose for each photo. We copped a plea that day, and my client learned a salutary lesson in the pitfalls of optimism bias.

Another classic example of this bias, and one that's very familiar to lawyers, is found in the domestic relations arena. The divorce rate in the United States is about fifty percent— one in every two marriages breaks up. Yet, as Sharot's research points out, you'd be hard pressed to find a newlywed couple who would categorically state their belief that their marriage will, likely as not, end in divorce. The news isn't all bad for lawyers: There's enough uncertainty among newlyweds to ensure a steady demand for prenuptial agreements. But the unfortunate truth is the belief of most newlyweds that they stand next to no chance of getting divorced, just like the belief of people who text while driving that they stand next to no chance of crashing, is a view that is divorced from reality.

As a cautionary note, I've found it's very possible in the negotiation context to harm your own chances of a favorable settlement by unintentionally fueling optimism bias in the other party. I have seen cases in which negotiators, hoping to cut to the chase, make a very reasonable first offer or demand. The other side, expecting the initial offer to merely be a starting point, becomes more emboldened by the prospect of coming out with a far better deal than was first imagined. As a result, the other party digs in its heels, and its counteroffer is far less favorable than it otherwise might have been. Social psychologists refer to this phenomenon as *anchoring*.

Think about this in the context of selling your house. You list it for $200,000, hoping that it will sell for $190,000. A potential buyer who is prequalified for a maximum of $190,000 comes in and offers $188,000. Suddenly you become very optimistic, and surmise that if the initial offer is that high, surely you'll be able to get more than the $190,000 you originally had in mind. You stick to your guns at full asking price, or a price slightly below it. The deal you gladly would have accepted had your optimism bias not kicked in now may well be lost.

I've seen this happen on any number of occasions when I've served as a mediator, and one party came in with a very reasonable first offer that the other side didn't expect. I've learned three key lessons from those experiences. First, I found it prudent to advise my clients in advance not to allow a reasonable initial offer from the other side to enhance their expectations. Second, I learned that it was preferable strategically to let the other side make the first offer so we could assess its reasonableness and couch our demand accordingly. Finally, I would ensure that the demand our side made was elevated, not so high that it would be viewed as foolish, but high enough so that it would not encourage any baseless optimism on the other side of the table.

The reason it's so important for us to be aware of optimism bias is simply that it's very helpful to know what it is that creates confidence in those who can cause us harm, and even more helpful to be cognizant of how easy it is for our own behavior to lead us down a dangerous path. That recognition won't shatter the optimism itself, but it will help us to manage potential risk by, perhaps, obtaining insurance, or making contingency plans to be prepared in the event that things go wrong.

Good guys or bad guys, most of us tend to be optimists. My colleagues and I are fully aware that every mole, every spy, every terrorist, and every criminal we've encountered has, to some degree, an optimism about him that many investigators might, perhaps foolishly, dismiss as arrogance or hubris. It's far more genuine than many would expect.

# Chapter 2

# SEEKING THE TRUTH, OR CONFIRMING WHAT WE BELIEVE IS TRUE?

||||||||||||||||||||||||||||||||||||||||||

How easy it might have been for Omar, with his trusted track record and devout faith, to slip past Phil, as he had done with so many other officers assigned to debrief him over the years. Phil fully expected the encounter to be a simple matter of confirming the conclusions of his predecessors. Fortunately, he was careful not to allow that expectation to sway him. He was well aware how easily we all can fall prey to *confirmation bias*—the tendency of people to believe information that confirms their expectations or preconceptions. Had Phil not checked any potential confirmation bias at the door, he might very well have been beaten.

Confirmation bias manifests itself in several ways. For example, we can actively seek out only the information that fits our preconceived notion of how something should be, ignoring evidence to the contrary. We may interpret a piece of information in a way that suits our view. Or we may hang on to a particular view, even after all the evidence points us in a different direction.

Anyone who has been through the detection of deception training conducted by QVerity, our consulting company, or who has read the book *Spy the Lie*, is well aware of the impact that confirmation bias has on our personal interactions with other people, and on our business transactions. In our training, we highlight how important it is to ignore truthful behaviors, and to instead focus on deceptive behaviors in the process of getting the truth. The reason is simple: Truthful behavior adds no value, and we need to filter out as much extraneous data as we can in order to be able to effectively analyze any deceptive behaviors a person may exhibit. Confirmation bias can hinder that process all too easily. In the case of Omar, there were a couple of decades of reports indicating that this was a man to be trusted, that this was to be a routine interview with a rock-solid asset. Confirmation bias may explain how Omar's deceit remained undetected for as long as it did. If we don't put that bias aside, we're easily inclined to form an initial impression, and to subconsciously seek out information that "confirms" that impression, often in the presence of contradictory information.

In the process of detecting deception, if we allow a first impression to suggest that someone is the "truthful type," our tendency is to leap on any truthful behavior we observe in order to bolster that impression. How many times have you heard a person say she believed what someone had said because of the job he does, or because of what she had heard about the person? That's confirmation bias. It causes us to seek out and interpret information in a way that supports our preconceived notions, whether that information is about a person, a company, a product, or virtually anything else—including, unfortunately, race, religion, nationality, and all the other distinctions that lead us to create stereotypes.

Watch any TV courtroom drama, or step into a courtroom during a trial, and you'll see lawyers using the concept of confirmation bias as a basis for a strong cross-examination. A great example is the phrase attributed to the late Johnnie

Cochran in the O. J. Simpson murder trial: "rush to judgment." Cochran accused the investigators of having made up their minds at a very early stage in the proceedings, and as a consequence, he said, they sought and interpreted evidence in a way that bolstered their view that Simpson was guilty of the murders of Nicole Brown Simpson and Ron Goldman.

Unless you check this confirmation bias at the door, you could fall victim to it, or to allegations that you're guilty of it. *"You made your mind up early on, and gave up looking at any other possibility, didn't you?"* is a powerful question, one I've used many times during cross-examination in civil and criminal cases. It's also a question that can only be genuinely refuted when you approach your search for the truth with an open mind, and you can demonstrate that you utilized an objective methodology.

Through years of representing victims of domestic violence, I've come to recognize that the damage that's done to the human psyche by physical and emotional abuse from someone the victim believes to be a loved one is unfathomable. It's a difficult situation to discuss, let alone observe. But it can serve as a poignant example of the power of confirmation bias, as so many of my clients truly believed that their abusers loved them. To me, it was a reflection of the purity of the hearts of many of my clients, and what I can only describe as the evil, twisted nature of their abusers.

One case in particular stands out. A client of mine, whom we'll call "Julie," was a very gentle, loving wife and mother. After years of abuse at the hands of her husband, whom we'll call "George," Julie was still desperate to keep her marriage intact for the sake of her six-year-old son. One evening, Julie went with George and their son to the home of their minister for marriage counseling.

When they arrived at the minister's home, George directed their son to run up and ring the doorbell. Still sitting in the car, Julie heard a distinct click from behind her. She turned around and was staring at two barrels of a shotgun. As she leapt from the car, George pulled the trigger. Miraculously, most of the pellets missed her, but some caused a deep wound to her left thigh. She fell to the ground, screaming in agony, "I've been shot! I've been shot!"

Lying on the ground crying, and with blood streaming from her thigh, she saw George looming above her with the shotgun. His next words to her were spoken with icy hatred: "That's not being shot, bitch. But this is." He pulled the trigger again. This time the blast removed most of her shoulder. George took off in the car, and was later caught by the police.

After several surgeries and a lengthy stay in the hospital, Julie came to my office. She was seeking a restraining order, as bail bonds set at that time, in that county, were notoriously low in "domestic" cases. This was such a case, even though George had been charged with attempted murder. Throughout our initial meeting, one thing struck me deeply. In spite of the years of torment, the physical and emotional abuse that culminated in an attack that could easily have killed her, Julie made a point of listing the "good" things that George had done. He had sent an apology through a relative, and made sure that their son received a birthday present. George, she believed, loved her. He had said as much. He had apologized, and he had sent gifts.

Julie had sought out the "evidence" that George loved her, and clung to that belief no matter how much evidence there was to the contrary. I cannot blame her. I cannot blame any victim of domestic or sexual violence, and I have no patience for anyone who does engage in victim blaming. I'm convinced that confirmation bias is so strong in so many of us, that even in horrific cases like Julie's, it can be extremely difficult to overcome. And I'm convinced that some people can, and do, prey on that. I also believe it's an oversimplification to suggest that confirmation bias is the exclusive driver of thought processes in domestic violence cases. Still, it was this case, and others like it, that led me to research confirmation bias to help me understand and better assist the victims I was representing.

What feeds confirmation bias, like many cognitive biases, is that we truly believe we're objective and open-minded, when in many cases we're really not. That's difficult for a lot of people to swallow, but there's an easy way to show how it happens.

When I teach negotiation classes, I use a very simple experiment developed by the psychologist Bertram R. Forer to illustrate confirmation bias—it demonstrates what's called the "Forer effect," sometimes better known as "Barnum statements." What I'm about to say will probably get me into hot water with those who are fans of TV mediums and psychics, but here we go. When you look at how this works, you'll see why so many purported psychics—and salespeople, for that matter—are believed, when what they're actually doing is making statements that could apply to almost anyone.

Forer's test is very simple to administer. All you have to do is come up with a fake personality test, and tell the people in the group that the resulting analysis will be unique to each of them. In truth, their answers are irrelevant, because the result you give them is this single analysis that Forer himself came up with:

> You have a great need for other people to like and admire you. You have a tendency to be critical of yourself. You have a great deal of unused capacity which you have not turned to your advantage. While you have some personality weaknesses, you are generally able to compensate for them. Your sexual adjustment has presented problems for you. Disciplined and self-

controlled outside, you tend to be worrisome and inse-
cure inside. At times you have serious doubts as to
whether you have made the right decision or done the
right thing. You prefer a certain amount of change and
variety and become dissatisfied when hemmed in by re-
strictions and limitations. You pride yourself as an independent thinker and do not accept others' statements
without satisfactory proof. You have found it unwise to
be too frank in revealing yourself to others. At times
you are extroverted, affable, sociable, while at other
times you are introverted, wary, reserved. Some of your
aspirations tend to be pretty unrealistic. Security is one
of your major goals in life.

As you can see, there are several statements in the results
narrative that could, and do, apply to almost anyone, yet they
are then qualified or even contradicted by others. If you ask
the people in the group to provide their assessment of the accuracy of the analysis, you'll find that across the board they'll
rate the results as highly accurate and applicable to them.
The reason is that their tendency is to seek out the positive
attributes. That confirms the positive things they think about
themselves, which in turn causes them to interpret the entire
analysis as an accurate reflection of their personalities. I, like
many negotiation trainers, have used this test in my classes
for years, and my students are invariably taken in by it.

The takeaway from this is just how important it is not to
allow confirmation bias to creep in when somebody is attempting to influence you by saying something positive about you.
I recall a particular case I handled, in which we were trying to
void a personal injury settlement that my client had agreed
to before seeking legal counsel.

As my client explained it, the other side had told him that
he was clearly someone who had good business acumen, and

while he had obviously been injured and was taking medication, that would not impair his ability to fairly and accurately discern the true value of his case. That conclusion was drawn from their "assessment" of my client's intellect following a review of his medical records. Anyone who would suggest otherwise was simply trying to "take advantage" of him.

In other words, *"We looked at some of your medical records, and now we would like to blow some smoke up whatever orifice it takes to convince you that you're completely capable of placing a value on a serious injury case. And if someone tries to convince you otherwise, he's a huckster."*

Unfortunately for my client, the bar is set very high on overturning settlements that have already been negotiated to a conclusion. He learned the hard way about the Forer effect, and about who was really taking advantage of him.

Back to Omar's case, he was relying, whether consciously or not, on Phil believing, based on years of positive reports, that he was an honest and trustworthy asset. He was likely confident that his demonstration of his devotion to his faith would confirm what he presumed was Phil's biased assessment of him. But Phil's ability to check his bias at the door meant there was no bias to confirm. In the end, what was confirmed instead was the effectiveness of Phil's approach.

# Chapter 3

# SHIFTING GEARS: FROM ASSESSMENT TO PERSUASION

‖‖‖‖‖‖‖‖‖‖‖‖‖‖‖‖‖‖‖‖‖‖‖‖‖‖‖‖‖‖‖‖‖‖‖‖‖‖‖‖‖‖‖‖‖‖‖‖‖‖‖‖‖‖‖

As Phil sat in the hotel room with Omar, he observed Omar's deception and knew that before him was a man who had spied on the United States and evaded detection for two decades. Phil had no doubt that this man posed a serious threat to U.S. security. But there was a cavernous gap between what Phil knew, and what could be proved. How Phil transitioned from listening and observing, to persuading Omar to tell the truth, would have a direct impact on the success of the encounter, and, ultimately, on the security interests of the United States. The stakes were extraordinarily high.

Whether you're trying to get someone to provide you with information he doesn't want to reveal, pay you money he'd rather keep for himself, or agree to the favorable terms you're seeking on a lease agreement, the *transition* is the point at which you move from the role of assessing what the other person has been saying to you, into the role of advocate, convincing the person to act honestly and in accordance with your aims.

In a negotiation situation, there are five stages in an effective, persuasive, and impactful encounter:

1) Preparation
2) Assessment
3) Persuasion
4) Exchange of proposals and options
5) Closing

Before coming to your meeting, it's essential to ensure that you're fully prepared (see Appendix II). Throughout the first portion of the meeting, you will have asked probing questions, listened, observed, and fully assessed what the other party has conveyed to you. Through your research prior to the meeting, and the information you gather during your assessment, you will have learned what motivates the other party, and what his interests are.

Now you're ready to employ your advocacy skills to persuade the other party to provide what you're seeking. In an elicitation situation, what you're seeking is the full truth. In a negotiation setting, it's the resolution you're aiming for. Many people believe that it takes years to become a skilled advocate. That's not the case at all. We all have the ability to formulate, and deliver, a persuasive argument. If we've done our preparation, and truly heard what the other side values, we can leverage that information to effectively persuade.

In the negotiation context, your persuasive statement—the negotiation equivalent of a monologue—should be detailed, balanced, concise, and sincere. Let's examine each of those elements:

## Detailed

Your statement should clearly outline each item that you want the other side to consider. Don't hesitate to bring photos, documents, or other exhibits to support your position. When negotiating for the purchase of a vehicle or other large item, written information about prices for these items elsewhere is good to have with you.

## Balanced

It's a fatal approach to be strictly one-sided, failing to recognize the validity of portions of the argument made by the other side. If you have information or evidence that contradicts what the other party has put forth, by all means, present it. But recognize the importance to them of what they have said—never dismiss anything out of hand. If the other side makes a point that you can't contradict, or a demand that costs you little or nothing, then concede to it.

## Concise

Concentrate on the matter at hand—don't recite facts that both sides are familiar with or that are uncontested. Don't bring extraneous matters like personal issues or criticisms into the discussion. You can easily lose the attention of the other party if you are insulting or demeaning, or if you take too long to present your side.

## Sincere

While a negotiation is not a plea to a jury, or to a group of voters, it is important that the other side see, and hear, your sincerity. If you become emotional in presenting your case, as long as it's genuine and not contrived, and it's within the bounds of social decorum (uncontrolled sobbing isn't likely to further your aims), don't be concerned. It can serve to authenticate your sincerity.

Finally, bear in mind that in order to effectively persuade the other party, it's essential to remain fully engaged throughout the entire encounter. Both parties need to feel confident that they have the attention of the other, and that everything they're saying is being heard. To that end, avoid all distractions and interruptions. Turn off your phone, and keep your laptop out of reach. And insist that the other party do the same.

# Chapter 4
# OH, TO BE LIKED!

||||||||||||||||||||||||||||||||||

"I like Foelandians," Lee said to Phil, explaining why he had been persuaded to work for the FIS. There is such potency, and such a lesson, in those simple words. It's the power of "liking."

Throughout this book, you'll notice a recurring theme: the importance of not making yourself an unlikable person. The "good cop, bad cop" routine is best left in Hollywood, for the reasons we've outlined. It all boils down to this: In an interview, an interrogation, a negotiation, a trial proceeding, a political campaign, or an everyday sales call, people learn that being liked—or, at the very least, not being *disliked*—is of paramount importance.

There is tremendous personal and societal pressure to say "yes" to, or do things for, people we like. Charities, businesses, intelligence operatives, and yes, even lawyers—all the good ones know the powerful force of a word, a smile, a kind gesture, a phone call.

As a lawyer, I learned early on from an attorney friend of mine, Jim Billings, to think of the world as a courtroom, and everyone in it as a potential juror—so winning over a jury began when I left my house in the morning. Jim taught me that wherever I went, I could potentially be seen by jurors in the case. The driver I cut off to grab the final parking space, the guy I let the door swing shut on, the woman who saw me ignore or be rude to a bailiff—in any of those situations, it could be a juror, or potential juror, who saw it, and that could torpedo my case. It was not that I wanted the jurors to like me, not that it wouldn't be a wonderful bonus if they did. It was just vitally important that I not be *disliked* by them.

I recall taking a deposition at the office of an opposing lawyer who was exceedingly frustrated with having to litigate our case. The deposition was being videotaped (back when we actually used videotape). The lawyer was becoming more and more exasperated, and kept interrupting my questions with a dramatic "Objection!" After this had happened several times, I asked him if he wouldn't mind waiting until I had completed my questions before objecting. His response to me was swift: "Listen, I'll object any goddamn time I feel like it!" I quickly replied, "Sir, please. There is no need for such vulgarity and profanity."

At the end of the deposition, when we were all packed up and about to leave, the opposing lawyer came up to me and apologized profusely for swearing.

"Peter, I'm really sorry," he said. "I didn't realize you'd be so offended."

"I wasn't at all offended," I replied. "I just don't do my swearing on the damn video." The point was simple: We were in the South, in the heart of the Bible Belt. Which one of us was more likely to be disliked by a judge or jury if they were to see the video?

On another occasion, just a week before Christmas one year, I was in probation court—the court where people appear when they're accused of violating the terms of their probation. If a violation is found, the penalty can run the gamut from a verbal rebuke from the judge to activation of a custo-dial sentence—that is, doing the time.

The judge on that day was Cliff Everett, a wonderful man who was known for his great sense of humor. As he came onto the bench, he said to all of the defendants assembled in the courtroom, "Ladies and gentlemen, it is one week before Christmas. Today, depending upon the circumstances of your case, you will be singing one of two songs: song one, "Blue Christmas," or song two, "I'll Be Home for Christmas."

Several defendants came through, pleading their cases and making their excuses. After a short while a middle-aged woman was brought up before the bench.

"Ma'am, what do you have to say for yourself?" Judge Everett asked.

"No excuse, Judge," replied the woman, who had clearly been through some hard times. "You go on and play that first song."

Laughter erupted from everyone in the courtroom, including Judge Everett. The woman had manufactured no excuse, and she made a joke at her own expense. After a short exchange, Judge Everett let her off with a stern warning, and she was indeed home for Christmas. The power of liking, and of honesty, had triumphed.

To fully appreciate the power of liking, we should also look at the case of Aldrich Ames, the most damaging Soviet mole in the CIA's history. Ames attributed his ability to deceive the Agency for so many years partially to the liking factor, which helped him pass polygraph examinations even when they indicated deception. In his book *The Spy Who Stayed Out in the Cold*, Adrian Havill wrote that Ames explained his success this way: "Confidence is what does it. Confidence and a friendly rapport with the examiner. You need rapport, where you smile and you make him think that you like him."

There are any number of factors that have an effect on the

degree to which someone is liked. Saying nice things to or about people goes a long way toward getting someone to like you. And you should be thankful that you're so good-looking. Research has shown that physically attractive people are more likely to be liked, and that people view them as having such likable traits as honesty, talent, and kindness. It speaks to the importance of being well-groomed and putting your best sartorial foot forward when engaging in any professional interaction.

The use of a person's name, especially the first name, can also positively influence familiarity and liking. Telemarketers and other salespeople routinely use this tactic. Once I caught on to it, I began to play a game with my wife, whenever we were making a major purchase, to count the number of times the salesperson used her first name, or mine. Like anything else, when it's overdone, it can appear fake, and it can backfire. But the subtle use of a person's first name can make him feel more relaxed, at ease, and cooperative.

I saw the positive effect of using a person's name from time to time in my law practice when I represented criminal defendants. On one occasion, I was representing a burglar I'll call "Jim Thomas." Though very prolific, Mr. Thomas was hopelessly inept, because he kept getting caught. When his day of judgment arrived, we were in court waiting to enter guilty pleas before a judge who, fortunately for Mr. Thomas, tended to be lenient. In the next courtroom was another judge, now a very well-known politician, who was known for genuinely being fair, kind, thoughtful, and courteous. However, when presented with guilty verdicts or guilty pleas in serious cases, he knew exactly how to throw the book, and he tended to throw it hard.

As luck would have it—all bad, it seemed, in my client's case—we were taken next door to appear before the other judge. Seeing that my client was in shackles, the judge instructed the bailiff to "remove Mr. Thomas's cuffs," because he was "presumed innocent and will be accorded that respect." The judge then ordered that the doors of the courtroom, which had been locked, be unlocked because these were the "people's courts to which access should not be restricted, and Mr. Thomas must know that justice can be seen to be done." By this point, my client had warmed tremendously to this judge, who had referred to him by name, and accorded him every respect.

We entered a guilty plea to two of four counts of burglary. The judge then read through the plea transcript, which involved asking my client a series of questions to ensure that his pleas were free and voluntary. With every question, the judge spoke in a calm, measured tone, often referring to my client as "Mr. Thomas," or "Jim."

The effect that had on my client was extraordinary. Although the judge imposed the well-deserved maximum sentence, my client's response was to thank the judge for treating him with dignity and respect. He walked out of the courtroom with a smile on his face.

"People don't often talk to me," my client said afterward. "Even in court, they just talk *about* me, and call me 'the defendant.'" It was clear he genuinely liked the judge who had just sentenced him.

Another behavior that can affect liking is unconscious familiarity. For example, a brief arm touch, as the research of Nicolas Guéguen and several other social psychologists has shown, can make the recipient like you more. Here, I urge caution, however. It can also appear strange, creepy, or downright assaultive if you linger too long in the touch. Touching someone's upper arm when you shake hands before a deposition or an interview can create a personal connection that can get things started in just the right way. The use of this technique by politicians was satirized in the movie *Primary Colors*.

Unconscious familiarity can also be leveraged through what's known in the field of negotiation and interviewing as *mirroring*. We tend to like people who are like us—those who are similar to us in background, opinion, lifestyle, or personality. This extends to similarities in movements and in behaviors—the crossing of one's legs, for example. But it obviously has to be done with extreme subtlety and discretion, so as not to come across as fake, or worse, mocking. Done effectively, it can be tremendously powerful.

When I would take depositions or conduct settlement negotiations in my office, I would always have done my homework on the background of the other parties. I would take the time to introduce myself and my office staff, perhaps give them a tour of the office, ask about their interests, and share a little of my own background and my likes, especially if there were any similarities between us. By the time we sat down for the deposition or negotiation, that bit of familiarity set the tone for a positive encounter. After all, think how connected you feel with someone you find, in the course of an interview, has a similar interest in a sports team or a travel destination, or who shares your views on politics or literature. This is a form of mirroring, and it can easily have an impact on you.

Have you noticed that every car salesperson you've ever purchased a vehicle from seems to love the same sports teams you do? I recently accompanied my wife when she set out to buy a new car. I noticed in a couple of dealerships that the offices of the salespeople were pretty bare. There were no posters or memorabilia that denoted a love of any particular team or sport. Why might that be? Could it be that a professed attachment to some college, some team, or some sport might make them less likable to us if we had attended a different college, or were fans of a team that was a fierce rival of the one they followed?

I once overheard a college fundraiser, whom we'll call "Henry," speaking with a wealthy male alumnus about sports. The alumnus, whom we'll call "Leonard," appeared to be an avid basketball fan, because the hat and shirt he was wearing promoted the college's basketball program. Henry mentioned how much he loved basketball, and that he followed the team with enthusiasm.

"Do you follow the girls team?" Leonard asked. Henry deduced from Leonard's use of the word "girls" that Leonard probably wasn't a huge fan of women's basketball.

"No," Henry replied. "I just don't think there is anywhere near the excitement in watching them play." It was a critical error in judgment. And it showed that Henry hadn't done his homework on this wealthy potential donor.

"Then you don't know my daughter," Leonard replied. "She plays on the team, and I think their games are even more exciting than the boys!"

The awkward backtracking that followed was excruciatingly entertaining. It was the face-to-face equivalent of trying to recall an embarrassing email that has already been sent. Henry fumbled his way through a horribly unconvincing response that he actually agreed that the women's team was indeed far more exciting and fun to watch than the men's. That only made matters worse, because it was so obvious that he was just sucking up to a wealthy alumnus. It wasn't a particularly effective way for Henry to boost his likability.

# Chapter 5
# TURNING "US AND THEM" INTO "WE"

||||||||||||||||||||||||||||||||||||||||

In many countries around the world, there are serious concerns about the legality of interrogation techniques that, on their face, are noncoercive, but that are viewed by courts as overreaching, or that could elicit false confessions. This is where there is a great utility and benefit in the methodology we utilize.

We talk elsewhere about the power of liking, and the impact of reciprocity on having people cooperate with you. Here, it's important to reiterate that our methodology involves the delivery of questions, and the monologue, in a very low-key, nonconfrontational manner. We are working with the subject, understanding his perspective, evincing that understanding, and guiding him to a point where he feels comfortable sharing information with us. There is never anything to be gained by coercing people in a way that can compel them to make false statements or confessions. That does nothing to further our aim of getting the truth, and it carries the serious risk of implicating the innocent, while allowing the guilty to walk free.

In a negotiation setting, working with the other party,

avoiding judgmental statements, and reflecting an understanding of their perspective, is what William Ury of the Harvard Negotiation Project, in his book *Getting Past No*, calls "stepping to their side." We want those on the other side of the table to view the negotiation as a situation in which they are working *with* us, rather than *against* us, to create a lasting resolution to the problem. As negotiators, we want to come away with the best result possible, and that often entails preserving a long-term relationship so that no bridges are burned, and our reputation as an ethical, effective negotiator is maintained.

Getting that positive result is rarely easy, but it can be aided tremendously by something as simple as asking, in a calm, measured tone, the question, "How do you think we can resolve this?" It's an incredibly powerful approach, because it's no longer an us-and-them scenario. We are now looking at how to resolve these issues together, side by side. It is far more effective than slamming a fist on the table, and angrily making a demand.

Taking a proposal that has been made by those on the other side, thanking them for it, and then patiently and calmly building on it can also be highly effective. Working with a proposal that comes from the other side as a foundation upon which to build a resolution is often the most expedient way to attain the result you were aiming for in the first place.

I was once engaged in negotiating the settlement of an "equitable distribution" case, a type of case that involves fairly dividing a couple's assets in a divorce proceeding. This case was especially complex, because it arose out of a grim domestic violence situation. In essence, we were utilizing a personal injury claim stemming from a very serious assault, in lieu of a traditional equitable distribution or spousal support case. In an equitable distribution case, my client could, at best, obtain fifty percent of the combined assets of her and her husband.

In a personal injury case, the amount she could receive was whatever a jury would award her. It was a gamble, but in light of the facts of the case, it was one well worth taking.

In these cases I would often meet with opposing counsel and his client, and have my client available on the telephone for input and instructions as needed. Such is the nature of domestic violence that putting a victim in the same room as the abuser often creates a coercive environment for the victim, and the other side prevails the vast majority of the time.

This was a case in which the husband—we'll call him "Andrew"—had not only controlled and mentally abused his wife, but had also physically assaulted her in the presence of their young child. Andrew was a wealthy professional, and my client, whom we'll call "Dorothy," was a stay-at-home mother who was planning (with Andrew's "permission") to return to college.

A proposal came from Andrew and his lawyer that he would transfer title to their house, and she would take over the mortgage. That was it. It was an offer that Dorothy would have wanted to reject out of hand. It was woefully inadequate, and did not address Dorothy's needs for affordable housing, support for herself while she got back into the workforce, support for her child, or an assurance that she and her child would be safe. It didn't even touch upon compensating her for the knife wounds and other injuries she had sustained from his attack.

Every fiber of my being wanted to tell this "man" what I thought of him, reject the offer, walk away, and go to trial. However, there was an opportunity. I needed to transition from where we were to a place where we could create an agreement.

Rather than reject the proposal, I reminded Andrew of the commitment he had made at the outset of the negotiation to work together to find a resolution in this case that would be fair to all involved, and would also demonstrate the love that he professed for his wife and his child.

Now, I had no sense of the degree of love he had for his child, but I certainly knew that the feeling he had for his wife had nothing to do with love. Regardless, he had made a commitment to work together with her, and to demonstrate what he claimed was his love. Together, "we" took his initial proposal and built on it. I guided that effort on Dorothy's behalf, calmly, without emotion, and by staying on message. As we began to construct each new iteration of the proposal, I would engage in a monologue that was very similar to the monologues we employ in an elicitation situation. I reminded Andrew of his commitment to work for a just, equitable resolution, and to act in accordance with his professed love of his wife and child. I reminded him that no marriage is perfect, that tempers fray, that emotions run high, and that sometimes things happen that we later regret. And I pointed out that sometimes we are presented with the gift of being able to rectify the wrongs, and make things right. The fact that I feel tremendous contempt for anyone who engages in domestic violence, which is inexcusable under any circumstances, had to be set aside.

By the end of the negotiation, Andrew had agreed to pay off the mortgage, and he signed the house over to Dorothy; thereafter, the house would go to their child. He agreed to a seven-figure lump-sum payment, and to a multiyear restraining order, with criminal and civil penalties built in for violations. The restraining order, which outlined the steps he had to take to make Dorothy feel safe, was far broader than any that a court would have granted after a trial.

The beauty of all of this was that it was Andrew's doing. He did it willingly, and each step along the way was taken in accordance with his initial commitment. William Ury describes this approach by referring to the instruction of Sun

Tzu: "Build your opponent a golden bridge to retreat across." He can claim victory, and take credit for the outcome.

There is a popular view that hard-as-nails, confrontational negotiators, like hard-as-nails, confrontational interrogators, get the best results with their arm-waving, table-banging, bellicose, in-your-face style. Nothing could be further from the truth.

Those tactics may work occasionally, but in the long term, people who negotiate or interact with these "hard" types are likely to become more entrenched, less willing to compromise, and more prone to responding in kind. Beyond that, people who are confronted with that behavior in a negotiation setting often spread the word about what they see as the person's obnoxious nature. Having hardball methods exposed to the public can be damaging in any number of ways.

Several years ago, an attorney I knew was going through a very rough time in his personal life. He was suffering from a bad bout of depression, and as a result he had failed to take some required steps in various legal proceedings on behalf of some of his clients.

Many attorneys understood this and, within the bounds of the ethics rules that require zealous representation of their clients, they found a way to work with the attorney and his clients to minimize the potential impact. Some attorneys, however, were of the take-no-prisoners variety, and decided to take advantage of the situation by seeking a default judgment—a judgment that is entered by the court when the other side in a case does not respond to the pleadings.

The court date arrived for the hearing by the judge of these motions for default, and the attorneys who were seeking them were lined up in court, salivating at the prospect of the favorable judgments they would receive.

When the first case was called, the judge looked at the lawyer seeking the default and said the following: "In all my years in practice, I have always believed that lawyers representing their clients should do what is right, what is just, and what is moral. That includes ensuring that the profession itself is not brought into disrepute through the use of 'win at any cost' tactics. A fellow member of the bar has found himself fallen on tough times. It is our duty to ensure that justice continues to be done, and be seen to be done. I will not be granting any default judgments today, and will remember those who come up here, to counsel's table, asking for one."

As if by magic, nearly every one of the hardball lawyers slipped out the back door of the courtroom, abandoning for that day their take-no-prisoners tactics. Who says there is no justice found in courtrooms?

# Chapter 6
# MONOLOGUES AND LEVERAGING THE POWER OF COGNITIVE DISSONANCE

||||||||||||||||||||||||||

In presenting a monologue, the aim is to help make the person feel good about himself, and to feel that he isn't being judged. That effort is bolstered by gaining an understanding of *cognitive dissonance*—the mental discomfort felt by a person who holds two conflicting ideas or beliefs simultaneously.

George Orwell, in his classic 1984, referred to the concept of simultaneously holding two conflicting beliefs as "doublethink." In Orwell's dystopia, doublethink created no discomfort, because people were oblivious to the conflict. In the real world, we're very much aware of it, and we tend to deal with the discomfort it causes by changing our thought processes. In a sense, we alter our perception of reality to explain away the conflict.

A popular illustration of cognitive dissonance, taught in business negotiation courses the world over, is given to us in Aesop's fable, "The Fox and the Grapes." In that story, a fox desperately wanted a deliciously tempting bunch of grapes that were hanging from a vine, just beyond his reach. Try as he might, the fox couldn't figure out a way to reach them.

When the fox realized there was no way he would be able

to get to the grapes, he had to reconcile the conflict that presented itself: He was a smart fox whose cunning ways had always gotten him what he wanted, yet he was outwitted by the mere location of the delicious grapes. So, rather than conclude that he was not as cunning as he thought he was, he decided that he didn't really want the grapes after all. He dealt with the dissonance by telling himself that the grapes were likely bitter, or sour—hence the phrase "sour grapes."

Anyone who commits a crime, misrepresents the facts, or tells a lie may put himself in a situation that forces him to deal with cognitive dissonance. Generally, the person is well aware that doing those things is wrong, and therefore bad. Yet he likely doesn't think of himself as a wrongdoer, or a bad person, so he's forced to reconcile these conflicting beliefs. In an interrogation situation, the monologue serves as a means of aiding that reconciliation in a way that's conducive to a confession, because it relieves the person of the mental discomfort that's caused by the dissonance.

The monologue is meant to prevent the person from focusing on the ramifications of the wrongdoing by keeping him in short-term thinking mode. We help him alleviate the pain he's feeling by giving him a remedy: a convincing argument, strengthened by rationalization, minimization, and socialization, that resolves the conflict. The resolution allows him to acknowledge the bad act, without having to accept the premise that he's a bad person.

Let's look at how this might work in a negotiation situation.

I once had a client who hired a contractor to construct a new office building. The project was "cost plus," meaning my client agreed to pay the cost of the construction plus a fee for the contractor, rather than agreeing on a set amount up front. After the job was completed, the cost that the contractor billed was far higher than what my client had anticipated.

As a result, a lawsuit was filed. At a mediation hearing convened to try to settle the suit, this is the way we approached the matter:

"Look, I know that in every business it's so easy to get swamped with work, and sometimes things just fall through the cracks or are missed, and sometimes we can miscount or miscalculate, or those who we employ as subcontractors can do the same thing. That's just the nature of being very good at what you do, because it makes you so busy that things can and do get muddled up. I think that may have happened here, because the figure you gave my client is vastly different from the figure that he had come up with when he priced this out. I wonder if it might be possible for us to take a step back, take a look at all of the bills from suppliers and subcontractors, and then look at the calculations again."

That approach led to a settlement that my client was pleased with. Chances are, if we had gone into the mediation and given the contractor the impression that we were calling him a liar or a cheat, we would have gotten nowhere. Rationalizing, minimizing, and identifying potential justifications all help to lower defenses that might otherwise make getting the truth next to impossible.

# Chapter 7

# RESISTANCE AND THE CONCEPT OF "COMMITMENT/ CONSISTENCY"

||||||||||||||||||||||||||||||

When the Chinese took American prisoners during the Korean War, they knew that they would face strong resistance in their efforts to get the Americans to provide information, or to willingly serve as conduits of propaganda. However, they were able to achieve many of their aims by means of a simple tool of influence that's extremely powerful in overcoming resistance. It's what the social psychologist Robert Cialdini refers to in his book *Influence: The Psychology of Persuasion* as *commitment/consistency*.

Rather than employ torture or other crude methods that were, at best, limited in their effectiveness, the Chinese, Cialdini points out, simply persuaded the Americans to make small concessions, in writing. Over time, the psychological impact of the concessions increased, and the prisoners' statements grew to be more and more reflective of sentiments that could be considered as pro-Chinese and anti-Western. The Chinese intelligence officers had tapped into a strong psychological driver: the desire people have to act consistently with their public statements and with the image of how they are perceived.

Recent political scandals, along with historical revision-ism on the part of political figures, have left many to wonder why some people will, often illogically, leap to the defense of those whose actions more sensibly warrant challenge, correction, or, heaven forbid, education. The answer is simple: the human desire, often unconscious, to appear to be consistent.

Many will recall that when former Alaska governor Sarah Palin visited Boston in 2011, she mangled the history of Paul Revere's ride. In her version of events, Revere wasn't warning the colonists of the approach of the British, but was warning the British that they'd better not take away the colonists' arms. In making a statement in support of Second Amendment rights, Governor Palin had dramatically altered a piece of American history that even schoolchildren know well. Despite the obviousness of the gaffe, she and many of her supporters later went to great lengths to defend what she had said, at one point contending that it was when he was detained by a British patrol that Revere had warned them against taking away the colonists' arms. She would later revise her explanation and fall back to insisting that there were some British in the area whom Revere was warning when he was making several rides and "ringing those bells." Throughout it all, many of her supporters stood by her version of events. The reason? Commitment/consistency.

Governor Palin had committed herself when she made that initial, off-the-cuff remark, and she refused to back down from it. The fear of appearing inconsistent in her statements trumped any concern of being shown to be wrong. Those who defended her had, in large part, backed her as a spokesperson for them and their values, and were committed to the consistency of their support despite the factual errors in her account.

The Irish writer and poet Oscar Wilde once said, "Consistency is the last refuge of the unimaginative." This wonderful reflection on our innate desire to conserve intellectual energy might help explain the psychology of commitment/consistency. Once someone commits to something, it's as if he goes on autopilot, following a course that can be viewed as consistent with that commitment. This has a huge potential impact on the way in which others can influence us, take advantage of us, and even use us for their own ends. Of course, it follows that it also has useful applicability in enabling us to influence others.

I focus heavily on this theory in negotiation classes as an example of why position-based bargaining is counterproductive. If you allow people to commit, especially repeatedly, to a particular position, they will become entrenched and will proceed to maintain, often unreasonably, a stand that's consistent with that position. The same is true when interviewing or examining a witness. The greater the extent to which someone is allowed to articulate a position, the more entrenched he becomes, and the more difficult it will be to sway him. Instead, it's best to identify an *interest* held by the other person that conforms to your own interests and purpose, allow him to openly acknowledge and commit to that interest, and then encourage him to act consistently in accordance with his interest-based commitment.

I recall once appearing before a judge with whom I had, to put it mildly, a frosty relationship. I was before him defending a motion, the loss of which would cost my client a considerable sum of money. There were two factors in my favor. First, the judge was running for a higher judicial office, and had made a campaign promise that was set in stone: He would not be an activist judge, one who "legislates from the bench." Second, to rule against my client, the judge would have to apply a novel, though not inconceivable, interpretation of the law.

I was fortunate in that the motion was the first matter of the day to be heard, and the courtroom was filled with lawyers, their clients, and the jury panel for that day. After the opposing counsel had finished his argument, I stood up, recited the rule to be interpreted, and made a statement that went something like this: "Your Honor, this is the rule, this is the plain English reading of the rule. To hold against my client, your Honor is being asked to rewrite this rule and to legislate from the bench. I am in your hands." I noticed the judge glance around the filled courtroom. Perhaps unsurprisingly, I won. My sense was that the judge's blood pressure was the loser that day.

No question, it is socially and politically desirable to be seen as consistent. Every U.S. politician dreads being labeled a "flip-flopper." The charge, in fact, can be a scathing insult. Cialdini cites a quote attributed to the nineteenth-century English chemist and natural philosopher Michael Faraday. When asked whether a rival chemist, whom he despised, was "always wrong," Faraday replied, "He's not that consistent." Indeed, being seen as inconsistent is sometimes more of an affront than being seen as wrong.

Keeping the commitment/consistency principle at the top of your mind can be very helpful in avoiding the trap of falling prey to those who would be inclined to use it against you. Have you ever noticed that highly effective salespeople have *you* fill out the contract or purchase order, especially when there is a cooling-off period that would allow you to cancel the contract? This approach is routinely taught in sales seminars, especially in states where cooling-off statutes have been enacted.

Similarly, in the legal realm, lawyers routinely have their clients fill out retainer contracts, writing in the prices and terms, initialing here, signing there. Is all of that really necessary? Yes, if you want them to be committed to the contract.

At the beginning of depositions, lawyers will ask deponents to agree that they will work with the lawyer to provide full and truthful responses, and to commit that if they are unclear about anything, they will stop the attorney and ask for clarification. The purpose is twofold.

First, asking for those commitments makes it very difficult for the deponent to come back later, when the deposition is over, and say that he gave a particular answer only because he didn't understand the question. If he does decide to give that a shot, it's very difficult for him to come up with a good response to the lawyer's next question: "But, Mr. Smith, don't you remember at the beginning of the deposition that you agreed that if you did not understand my question, you would ask me, then and there, for clarification?"

Second, the deponent has committed to be truthful and co-operative. If, during the course of the deposition, he becomes in any way obstructive or defensive, we remind him of his commitment, and simply ask him to act in a manner that is consistent with it.

I've also found this to be a tremendously useful tool in negotiation and mediation. At the outset, I ask the other side to commit to work with me honestly and constructively. In some cases I have even written up short agreements that we all sign, stipulating that we all agree to be fair and truthful. The results that I've seen this small gesture yield are amazing.

In the classroom, too, I have utilized this commitment strategy to encourage students to complete all work assigned for a course. One course I taught required students to watch a series of video lectures online. I had the students sign an agreement that they would watch all of the lectures, and that if they didn't do so, they would fail the course, regardless of how well they performed on the tests. After the final exam, one student, who had aced the exam, came up to me and said, "Look, I did really well on the tests. Is it okay if I don't watch the last lecture?" I took out his "contract" and showed it to him. He nodded, and left to watch the lecture.

It's essential, then, to stay on the offensive side of the commitment/consistency line. In depositions, in negotiation, in mediation, even when buying a house or a car, your aim should be for the person on the other side of the table to commit that he will act fairly and abide by the rules. If the circumstances allow for it, get him to agree to having you both sign a written statement to that effect. Then, if he strays from that path, you can politely remind him of the commitment you both made at the outset.

# Chapter 8

# SLOW AND STEADY ACROSS THE GOLDEN BRIDGE

||||||||||||||||||||||||||||||||||||||||||||||||||

The admonition to check your progress as part of a structured approach to an elicitation situation is just as applicable to business and personal negotiation scenarios. It's essential to allow the person on the other side of the table to work with you in a manner that enables you to gather the information you need in order to assess his position at any point in the negotiation process.

Recall in my Chapter 5 commentary the case of Andrew and Dorothy, where we built Sun Tzu's "golden bridge" by using a proposal by Andrew as the foundation in the equitable distribution proceeding. Just as a guilty suspect doesn't necessarily plan to confess when he steps into the interrogation room, what Andrew had envisaged when he sat down at the negotiation table was likely a far cry from what he eventually agreed to. Getting there required patience and a systematic means of reading the situation.

Imagine what might have happened if, as soon as Andrew had committed to negotiate fairly as a demonstration of love for his wife and child, I had said, "Okay, then give them the house, sign a multiyear restraining order, and pay them a large lump sum of money." Chances are, we would have gotten absolutely nowhere. Instead, we needed to proceed at a slow and steady pace, posing noncoercive questions: "What do you think would be fair?" "Would you consider doing this?" "Wouldn't it be great for your son if you did that?" This is the negotiation equivalent of asking, "What else?" You continue to add foundation blocks for your golden bridge until you've done all you can do.

Be aware that it's far too easy to pounce when you get the admission or concession you were seeking. More often than not, he shoots himself in the foot. When you see that your monologue is having a positive effect, proceed with care and ensure you're not jumping the gun when you decide to check your progress. Let the person cross that golden bridge at his own pace, on his own accord. Trying to rush him across will almost certainly cause the bridge to collapse.

# CHAPTER 9

# THE FICTION ROUTE CAN BE DANGEROUS, SO PROCEED WITH CAUTION

||||||||||||||||||||||||||||||||||||||||||||||||||

Highlighting a shared experience can be remarkably effective in creating a bond with another person. As has been discussed elsewhere, we're more likely to cooperate with people we like, and who are like us. So a shared background or a shared loss, for example, can establish a connection that encourages people to provide truthful information.

When selecting juries, seasoned trial lawyers often will, within the bounds allowed by the judge, share information about themselves or their clients with each potential juror. Since juries are more likely to side with the lawyer and client they can more easily identify with, this simple gesture can yield very positive results. It is, of course, essential to observe applicable laws and codes of conduct with respect to the factual nature of the information being shared. This applies equally to interview, elicitation, and negotiation situations.

For example, in the United States, law enforcement officers can legally misrepresent certain matters when interviewing a suspect in a criminal case. The police may tell a suspect that a codefendant has confessed and implicated him when he hasn't, or that they have incriminating fingerprint or DNA evidence when in reality no such evidence exists. They cannot, however, make a misrepresentation to a suspect about a deal, such as an assurance that he'll receive a lighter sentence if he confesses, when that's not the case. In some other countries, any misrepresentation by law enforcement is prohibited.

Similarly, in negotiations, lawyers are bound by rules of professional conduct found in American Bar Association Model Rule 4.1, which requires that they not "make a false statement of material fact" to a third party during their representation of a client. Any party in a negotiation, solicitation, or business transaction, moreover, is well advised to take extreme care to avoid making any untruthful claims. For example, if someone were to make a statement about a relative dying of a certain disease as a means of persuading people to donate to a particular charity, he may well find himself on the wrong end of a felony prosecution. So it's essential to always be mindful that going the fictitious route can take you into extremely dangerous territory, especially if the fiction can easily be tested. It can completely undermine your credibility, and destroy your ability to effectively engage with the person sitting across the table.

It's equally essential to ensure that your delivery is absolutely clear, since it's very easy for someone to take something you say out of context, or to mischaracterize it in a way that bolsters his own position. I recall an occasion in which I represented a police officer who made a statement during an interview that he had "been on firearms training with the SWAT team." The questioner returned to that statement later in the interview with this contention: "Earlier you claimed that you were on the SWAT team. That was a lie! You were never in SWAT, you never even applied for SWAT." The questioner was furious, and appeared to be grasping at anything he could to make his case. The fact was, my client had never suggested he was on a SWAT team, or that he had ever applied. He merely mentioned that he had attended firearms training with the SWAT team. That the questioner had jumped to an erroneous conclusion served as a reminder of the importance of delivering your message clearly, and in a way that doesn't lend itself to mischaracterization.

Conveying a fictitious account of some dimension of your background or experience, in order to demonstrate sincerity and empathy in an elicitation situation, can be an effective means of creating a bond that will encourage a person to reveal the truthful information you're seeking. But it's a tack that must be taken with great care and prudence. Whenever possible, it's likely in your best interest to create that bond on the strength of your authentic experiences. That approach can reduce the risk of stepping over a legal or ethical line that you never want to cross.

# Chapter 10
# "THOSE TO WHOM EVIL IS DONE"
||||||||||||||||||

If there's one thing that very few people like, it's being judged. Someone who feels that others are sitting in judgment of him is very likely to react with defensiveness and rancor—a reaction that in an elicitation or negotiation situation needs to be avoided at all costs. Consider Michael's interrogation of Tommy, the live-in boyfriend. In spite of the horrific injuries Tommy inflicted on the baby girl, Michael made it crystal clear that he wasn't judging Tommy. That approach not only avoided a defensive reaction, it also helped to keep Tommy in short-term thinking mode. Being judged in Tommy's situation would carry with it a connotation of legal consequences, and Michael clearly had to prevent Tommy's head from going there. It was no accident that when Tommy asked Michael what he would do in that situation, Michael's response was, "I would tell the truth," not "I would sign a confession," or "I would admit my guilt."

The admonition, "Judge not, that ye be not judged," is worthy of remembrance. One of my favorite poems of all time is "September 1, 1939" by W. H. Auden. In it there is part of a verse that I have printed out and posted in my office, and that

I would often carry with me on business to admonish me to sit in judgment of no one, and to regulate my temper and my conduct when conducting interviews, negotiations, and depositions. It reads, simply:

> I and the public know
> What all schoolchildren learn,
> Those to whom evil is done
> Do evil in return.

These words reinforce what we have discussed earlier about the power of liking, and the criticality of not being disliked. They also teach us about the tremendous impact of the principle of reciprocity: That which we do to others, or that which others perceive we have done to them, may well be done to us, good or bad.

A classic example of reciprocation for perceived bad treatment was demonstrated at the beginning of World War II. At the end of World War I the Allies used a railroad car as the venue for the signing of articles of surrender that were considered by the Germans to be extremely harsh and humiliating. More than two decades later, when the Nazis defeated the French, they had the same railroad car removed from a museum, and forced the French to sign articles of surrender in it. It was clear that their use of the railroad car was payback for what had occurred all those years earlier.

If Phil, Michael, or Susan ever approached their elicitation encounters with a heavy hand, the overbearing "bad cop" routine that's so frequently portrayed in movies, those they questioned likely would have clammed up or responded to them in kind.

For many years, I have represented and advised law enforcement officers, typically in cases where there was an investigation surrounding the use of lethal force. I witnessed firsthand the impact of different questioning styles on my clients. Those investigators who came in primed for confrontation would quickly earn my client's distrust, and mine as well. Those who came in with a more relaxed, friendlier approach would quickly gain our respect and confidence, and often our trust.

I learned from one of my mentors a wonderful technique for setting the stage for a highly productive negotiation: Bring food—doughnuts, cookies, sandwiches, it really doesn't matter. It's easy and cheap, and it's effective because it leverages two key principles of influence. The first is simply that people are more responsive to persuasion when they're eating, perhaps because they associate eating with a pleasurable experience. The second is that you're doing something nice for them. That not only makes you likable, psychologically it causes the person to feel indebted to you.

When I served as an honorary consul, my primary responsibilities were business-oriented and largely ceremonial in nature. My duties included introducing diplomats to government officials or business executives, and conducting introductions between businesses overseas and in the United States. One of the things that always intrigued me was how many of these, and other high-level meetings, took place over lunches or dinners, and that it was almost always the side seeking concessions or that had the most to gain from the encounter that would declare up front that it was hosting the meeting. Being liked, and creating that sense of indebtedness, were quite valuable in the high-stakes worlds of diplomacy and international business.

The very same principle applies in the case of the car dealership that offers a "free" breakfast when you come in for a test drive, the time-share facility that offers you "free" tickets to a theme park, or the survey company that sends you a dollar bill in the envelope with a survey it wants you to complete.

The result in each case is the same: You're likely to feel indebted, and a desire to reciprocate the kindness.

People often don't expect the kindness you show them—in many cases, they fully expect the opposite behavior, which can make a kind gesture even more effective. Those on the other side in a court case, interrogation, or negotiation may well expect you to come on strong, with a take-no-prisoners approach. They'll be disarmed by your kindness, and many will respond in kind. In any case, they'll find it much more difficult to dislike you.

During a negotiation, I would always thank the other party for any concessions that were made. In depositions, I would express my appreciation for the person's cooperation, and for his responses. I recall one deposition in particular that ended with the following exchange:

**Me:** Thank you, sir, for coming here today, for accommodating my client's schedule, and for providing such thorough answers. You have been very kind.
**Deponent:** No problem. This was actually pretty easy, and, if I'm being honest, not what I expected. In fact, I thought you would be a real asshole.
**Me:** Well, thank you again. And honestly, it takes people knowing me for several months before they realize that I am indeed a real asshole.

We laughed at that together—at that moment, we weren't adversaries, we were just two people sharing a joke. Regardless of all of the legal proceedings, we were suddenly on the same side—the side of humor. We parted company as we had met, in a friendly fashion. The case settled a few weeks later.

On another occasion, I represented a woman who had been the victim of some of the most disturbing acts of domestic violence I had become aware of in handling more than 1,200 cases of domestic violence and sexual abuse. Over the years, this woman had been cut with knives and box cutters, had cigarettes stubbed out on her skin, and had been slammed against furniture, walls, and doors by her husband—all in front of their son. Before I met him, I hated him.

In a meeting with the husband, his lawyer, the prosecutor, and the arresting officer, we had two matters to discuss: his plea in the case of assault on a female; and the entry against him of a domestic violence protective order. I had seldom met such an arrogant, rude, and offensive man; as far as I was concerned, he was human detritus. Yet I came into the meeting with a box of doughnuts I had purchased outside the courthouse from a merchant whose proceeds, ironically, supported a shelter for victims of domestic violence.

Knowing that I was representing his wife, the husband expected me to hate him, and to behave angrily toward him. It took every ounce of self-restraint that I had (and I am not known for my self-restraint), but my demeanor was cordial and polite. The upshot of the conference was that the defendant agreed to plead guilty as charged, and consented to a protective order that included my client having residency in and possession of the family home, custody of their minor child, and child support. These are certainly all things that would have happened at trial, but my client was spared that ordeal. Was it all because of some doughnuts? Probably not. However, had I exhibited the anger and aggression I was truly feeling, rather than the kindness and respect I showed him, it is far less likely that the defendant would have agreed to anything at the meeting. The outcome for my client would have been a painful trial, and further anguish.

Don't be concerned that your kindness, or speaking calmly, will be seen as a sign of weakness, or a lack of confidence. Just the opposite is the case—it demonstrates that you have the utmost confidence in your abilities, and that you don't have to resort to aggression or bullying tactics to get your way.

A final bit of advice if you find yourself in a negotiation or sales situation, and you're on the receiving end of unexpected kindness, "free" gifts, or generous hospitality. Take a step back and recognize it for what it might be. Ensure that any concession or offer you make is one you would have made anyway.

# Chapter 11
# WALKING A MARINE
# THROUGH A MINEFIELD
||||||||||||||||||||||||||||||||||||||||||||||||||

When the investigators who initially interviewed Ralph used the word "molested" to characterize what they were accusing him of doing to Judy, they handicapped themselves by making it extremely difficult to get the truth from Ralph. The use of such a harsh term, one that carries a stigma with life-altering consequences, gave Ralph every incentive to do everything in his power to conceal the truth.

Ralph was very much aware that he had engaged in inappropriate sexual activity with a sixteen-year-old girl. Yet he very likely thought of himself as a good person—a United States Marine who had served his country, and who was now serving his community as a law enforcement officer. He also knew full well that good people don't "molest" children. So he had a conflict in his mind that had to be reconciled before there was any chance of him revealing the truth.

Being labeled as someone who had "molested" Judy almost certainly caused Ralph to dislike his accusers, which decreased the chances of a confession even further. Beyond that, the use of the term made it clear to Ralph that the investigators were judging him, and that anyone who would judge him in that way could never understand what had happened in that truck. Their aim, as he saw it, was to end his career and ruin his life by throwing him in prison. Telling them the truth under those circumstances wasn't an option.

It was only when Michael came in that a pathway to the truth was opened. No doubt, that pathway weaved through a minefield for this Marine, so it was up to Michael to keep Ralph's mind off the potentially explosive nature of every step they took. With his easygoing style and low-key manner, Michael was able to engage Ralph and, more important, gain his trust. This all served to reduce the dissonance that Ralph was experiencing, and to get him to a place where he was ready to open up.

The questions Michael asked regarding what Ralph was feeling are instructive not only in an interrogation situation, but in a negotiation setting, as well, as we seek to ascertain what's driving the other person's position. Understanding what motivates someone in that position, and what he would most want or fear, can be an invaluable guide in creating options and making proposals that can lead to a resolution.

A key nuance of the interrogation was that although Michael downplayed the consequences that Ralph brought up, at no point did he say that Ralph might be let off the hook, or that there would be no negative outcome. By shifting Ralph's thinking from the worst-case scenario to the positive nature of cooperation and admitting his wrongdoing, Michael was able to plant that mind virus, and leave it to Ralph to take it wherever he wanted to go.

When it was time for Michael to check his progress, he did so not by demanding that Ralph confess, but rather by strategically using a presumptive question: "Was it her idea?" Then, as Ralph opened up, there was no gloating, no judging, no criticizing on Michael's part. He stayed on course and carefully guided Ralph the rest of the way through the minefield and into the hands of his superiors.

There's a valuable lesson in Michael's refusal to gloat or pat himself on the back when he got the truth from Ralph. William Ury's counsel to heed Sun Tzu's admonition to build a golden bridge for the other person to retreat across suggests an equally worthy piece of advice: Never burn that bridge by being overly proud of your accomplishments.

In a case I once handled as a mediator, both sides had tentatively agreed to a settlement—one that I felt was reasonable and good for all concerned. We were to come back the next morning to finalize the agreement and sign the settlement papers. Unfortunately, one of the individuals decided to throw a party that night to celebrate his "big win." Word of the party got back to the other side, and the next morning, the deal was off. No matter how reasonable the terms of a settlement appear to be, no one wants to be branded as the loser. In the end, the side that had celebrated its "big win" came away with a far less attractive settlement.

# Chapter 12

# NEGOTIATOR, INTERVIEWER, OR INTERROGATOR, YOU'RE PLAYING A ROLE

||||||||||||||||||||||||||||||||||

In December 2008, Clark County, Nevada, District Court Judge Jackie Glass sentenced O. J. Simpson to up to thirty-three years in prison, following his conviction on charges stemming from an attempted robbery in Las Vegas in September 2007. It was the maximum sentence Judge Glass could impose. Simpson won't be eligible for parole until 2017.

This time, Simpson did not publicly assert that he was "absolutely, one hundred percent, not guilty," as he did after being charged with the murders of Nicole Brown Simpson and Ron Goldman. Rather, after being confronted with recordings of the incident and other damning evidence, he maintained that he had been trying to recover sports memorabilia that belonged to him. One cannot help but wonder whether Simpson would have taken a similar tack had he been presented with the damaging evidence against him on the day after the murders. Instead of insisting that he had nothing to do with the murders, would he have felt compelled to admit his involvement, and have decided that his only course of action was to try to somehow justify it? We can only speculate.

As we have stated, it is not our intent to demean anyone

who was involved in handling the Simpson murder case. Observers have faulted the prosecution for a variety of reasons, including its failure to present certain evidence during the trial. But the case can never be retried, so all of that is moot. For some, there is consolation in the fact that Simpson was found liable in a civil case, resulting in a judgment against him of over $33 million. That might have been some consolation to the Brown and Goldman families, but it no doubt did very little to lessen their grief.

Perhaps they felt some sense of consolation, as well, when Simpson was finally put behind bars following his sentencing in Nevada. The image of Simpson sitting, at long last, in a stark prison cell is one that many see as having come thirteen years later than it should have. In the hypothetical situation we presented, would the outcome of Michael's interrogation of Simpson have been a one-way ticket for the jet-setting celebrity to a room with no view at Pelican Bay State Prison? I would submit that it very likely would have.

The hypothetical confession obtained by Michael is one that would stand up in any court in the United States, and, indeed, in most jurisdictions around the world. Simpson was read his Miranda rights, and was interviewed in a manner that was neither unethical nor coercive. Michael's demeanor was calm, low-key, and nonconfrontational.

In the course of the interrogation, Michael convinced Simpson that he *understood* him—that he could imagine how difficult it was for him to deal with the "bad Nicole" that had emerged since their divorce. Many might come away from reading what Michael said to Simpson during the hypothetical interrogation, and ask how he could possibly depict Nicole in such a negative light, and seemingly justify the brutal murders. It's a question that warrants examination.

When I was growing up in England, I spent a lot of time visiting my father's office. He was a lawyer, and later a judge. I once asked him why lawyers wore wigs and robes in court. He said there were many reasons, some historical, but that one that resonated with him was that they were playing a role, and this was their "costume." When they put on the costume and stepped into court, they put aside their personal beliefs, biases, and emotional attachments, and they took on the role of advocate for their client. This is how they managed to effectively represent clients they personally found to be repugnant. In their costume, they were not personally attached to, or associated with, the arguments they made. They could make arguments that, though inconsistent with their personal feelings, could effectively serve the requirements of the law, and of justice.

When we step into an interview or an interrogation, we are stepping into a role. Could Michael, or any of us, have possibly believed that Nicole, or Ron Goldman, bore any responsibility whatsoever for their tragic deaths that night? Of course not. But had Michael failed to communicate some sense of understanding and empathy with respect to what may have driven Simpson to commit the acts that brought him to that interrogation room, getting the truth from Simpson would almost certainly have been futile.

Similarly, in a negotiation setting, the best negotiators find ways to put the other party at ease, to take personality conflicts out of the mix, and to arrive at a favorable resolution. In a business transaction, dealing with a slimy salesperson, or an unethical corporate executive, requires us to don our metaphorical wigs and robes, and to play our role. Even in a family dispute, assuming a role that entails genuine consideration of all viewpoints, and detachment from a hard-nosed, win-at-any-cost position, can yield results that everyone is comfortable with, and that previously might have seemed nearly impossible to achieve.

# Chapter 13
# THE ENDGAME
||||||||||||||||||||||||||||||||

Our approach to elicitation mirrors our approach to any business or personal interaction that involves conflicting agendas. It's essential to understand what motivates the other party, and to apply that understanding in a calm, structured, ethical manner. Using a methodology that builds rapport and strengthens relationships, rather than one that relies on coercion or threats, leads to more reliable information being obtained, better deals being reached, and more trusting relationships being built. As W. H. Auden reminded us, those we harm are likely to do harm to us in return, be it in the form of refusing to cooperate, providing information of suspect value or veracity, or causing a reputation to be forever damaged.

In his book, Ali Soufan highlights the fact that Boris was woefully ill-prepared, both in terms of understanding Abu Zubaydah's background and motivations, and in terms of how to conduct an effective interrogation. Yet it was clear that that fact completely eluded Boris. Research by David Dunning and Justin Kruger has identified this cognitive bias, now known as the "Dunning-Kruger effect"—it manifests itself when people of limited capability in a given area suffer from the illusion that they have much greater skills in that area than is actually the case. Those who are ill-prepared or incapable can fail to recognize just how ill-equipped they truly are. This was certainly the case with Boris.

Who among us, when enduring physical or emotional pain or torment, would not do all in our power to make that torment stop? Under such agonizing circumstances, we admit to and apologize for things we haven't done, and we make up things that we think people want to hear. This is why blackmail and extortion are punished so severely in criminal law: Subjecting people to this form of emotional torment can cause them to do things they would otherwise never do. Boris was absolutely right when he said, "It's human nature to react to these things." But what he was unable to comprehend was that the information yielded by the reaction might well be entirely meaningless.

Examining Boris's lack of preparation and his blunt force methods, compared to Frank's fully prepared and systematic approach, is like watching two carpenters build a fine piece of furniture, one with nothing but a hammer and having no idea what he's building, and the other with a full set of tools and a detailed design schematic. Who is more likely to have a better outcome?

Throughout this book, we have discussed this more finessed approach in interviews, in negotiations, indeed in life. Like all things of great value, it requires tremendous preparation and great effort. But the outcome pays huge dividends. By taking a noncoercive, ethical approach, we stand a much better chance of getting the truth. And we're far better equipped to create lasting relationships that can help us attain our personal and professional goals.

## Appendix II

# IT ALL BEGINS WITH PREPARATION

||||||||||||||||||||||||||

### By Peter Romary

One of the essential keys to effective interviewing, elicitation, advocacy, and negotiation is to be fully prepared for the task ahead of you. Let's look at preparation from two perspectives: active practice, and information collection.

## ACTIVE PRACTICE

In preparing for any kind of encounter, it's essential to recognize that there is no substitute for actual practice. Just as you would never perform surgery after simply reading a textbook on surgical techniques, you can't assume that reading this book, or any other book, will adequately prepare you for a situation in which your aim is to get the truth. As with any other skill, you need to practice what you have learned on a regular basis.

I can well remember the very first big criminal case that I was to try as a lawyer. I was fresh out of law school and was appointed to represent a defendant on a very serious felony charge (thankfully the representation-by-rookie scenario is no longer possible in the state where I live). I performed research, interviewed witnesses, studied the case law, learned about the presiding judge, and familiarized myself with my client's codefendants. The one area where I was lacking was in actually trying cases before juries. I had studied trial advocacy in law school, and tried mock cases before mock juries, but I had yet to do it where it mattered.

To overcome this problem, I enlisted the assistance of two mentors. The first one, who had been practicing for a couple years and who was, in my eyes, a savvy veteran of the criminal courts, sat with me for jury selection. We got through that process with very little trouble, and with plenty of pointers from my mentor I felt nearly invincible. During a short recess before the opening statements, I turned to my trusted advisor.

"This is going great!" I said enthusiastically. "Now that you've seen the jury, what suggestions do you have for my opening statement?"

"I'm not sure," he replied. "I've never gotten past this point in a jury trial." It turned out that my mentor was indeed an experienced criminal defense lawyer, but only in district court, where cases are tried before judges, not juries.

Fortunately, the second lawyer who was mentoring me, a seasoned pro in jury trials, arrived. He didn't bother to contain his laughter when he saw the look on my face and I told him about my predicament. In the end, I received a reprieve: The district attorney came over and said that based on evidence gathered from a codefendant, they were dismissing the felony charges against my client. It was way too close for comfort, but it taught me a lesson I've never forgotten: Relying on someone else's skills, rather than concentrating on developing your own, can be disastrous.

I'm frequently chided by colleagues for the fact that I tell my students to ignore anyone who says to them, "Wait until you get out into the real world." That's nonsense. We're not playing roles in *Avatar*—we were born into the real world, and we're in situations where we have to interact, resolve conflicts, assess credibility, and persuade others every day. So it's best not to rely on "experts," but rather to practice your skills at every opportunity.

## INFORMATION COLLECTION AND ONLINE RESEARCH

The second area of preparation involves collecting as much information as you can so you know the party you're dealing with inside and out.

A law school mentor of mine in England, Professor John Murdoch, told me that to be really good as a negotiator or an advocate, I needed not only to know the facts of my case, but also to be able to step into the shoes of the other party and know the facts of his case, as well as his perspective of his own case, and of mine. I have carried that advice with me, and I've found it has broad application in many arenas.

How effective would an interrogator be if he didn't understand the religious, political, or ideological motivations of the person he was tasked to interrogate? That background information is crucial fodder for the construction of an effective monologue. Similarly, how successful would a negotiator likely be if she didn't understand what interest the other party was attempting to serve in making his demands?

For a number of years I have worked in the field of threat management, with a concentration in the area of higher education. The aim is to collect information that can be used to prevent people from harming others, harming themselves, or harming property. A key skill in threat management, as in litigation and negotiation, is the ability to quickly, ethically, and effectively collect information about individuals who may pose a threat. My good friend and colleague, Dr. Jeff Pollard, a highly regarded clinical psychologist and expert in threat management, uses a wonderful phrase to describe the process of creating an assessment of an individual: "Before we can *connect* the dots, first we have to *collect* the dots."

There are several key places to look in the process of collecting those dots. They include, but are not limited to, the following:

- Criminal records
- Civil judgment records
- Sex offender registries
- Credit records (subject to appropriate authorization)
- Tax records
- Real estate transfer and ownership records
- Social media presence

In the social media category, there are a number of Web sites that are especially helpful resources in providing background information on individuals. I've worked with two highly respected colleagues in the threat management field, Dr. Marisa Randazzo and Dr. Gene Deisinger, to put together a list of sites that indicate how individuals are represented, and how they represent themselves, online. Working with students has taught me that it's important to cast the net more widely than a lot of people would expect. Younger people have a presence on many social media sites that many older people have never even heard of. So, as you seek out information, ask questions of others about where you should be looking online.

The sites we use as resources include:

- Archive.org
- Avvo
- Blogger
- Craigslist (search relevant city/town)
- Facebook
- Foursquare
- FriendsReunited
- Google/Yahoo!/Bing (search engines through which you should search for names, e-mail addresses, and phone numbers)
- Google+
- Instagram
- LinkedIn
- MySpace
- Ning
- Pheed
- Pinterest
- RateMyProfessors
- Reddit
- Snopes
- Technorati (searches blogs)
- Tumblr
- Twitter
- Vine
- WordPress
- Xanga
- YouTube

The information that we collect from these online searches, in addition to what we're able to glean from simply talking to people, can be invaluable in creating an accurate portrayal of the kind of person or company we're dealing with. No interview, elicitation, or negotiation situation should ever be entered without having as much relevant background information as you can possibly gather on the person sitting across from you. Failure to gather that information can undermine your effectiveness and make your desired outcome—be it the truth, a favorable settlement, or a great deal—far more difficult to secure.

## Appendix III

# TRANSCRIPT OF THE ACTUAL INITIAL INTERVIEW OF O. J. SIMPSON

||||||||||||||||||||||||||||

### Conducted by LAPD Detectives Philip Vannatter and Thomas Lange

### June 13, 1994

NOTE: As you read through the transcript, consider the following questions:

- Had the detectives properly prepared for the interview?
- Did they come into the interview with a clear strategy and a goal they hoped to accomplish?
- Did they establish individual roles for themselves prior to the interview, and conduct the interview accordingly?
- Did they lock Simpson into a clear alibi?
- Were they able to get Simpson to commit to a specific timeline for his activities the night before, and particularly between the hours of nine and eleven, when investigators determined the murders were likely committed?

- Did they obtain a coherent reason for how Simpson sustained the wounds to his left hand?
- Did they properly explore and clarify contradictory statements?
- Did they focus on high-value questions, or did they become distracted by pursuing irrelevant and meaningless lines of inquiry?
- Did they waste precious time asking background questions that could easily have been addressed elsewhere?
- Did they display an appropriate demeanor, or were they overly deferential to Simpson?
- Did Simpson leave the interrogation room having learned more information about the case than the detectives learned from him?
- *Did they ask the most important question of all, whether he caused the deaths of Nicole Brown Simpson and Ron Goldman?*

**Vannatter:** . . . my partner, Detective Lange, and we're in an interview room in Parker Center. The date is June 13, 1994, and the time is 13:35 hours and we're here with O. J. Simpson. Is that Orenthal James Simpson?

**Simpson:** Orenthal James Simpson.

**Vannatter:** And what is your birth date, Mr. Simpson?

**Simpson:** July 9, 1947.

**Vannatter:** Okay, prior to us talking to you, as we agreed with your attorney, I'm going to give you your constitutional rights. And I would like you to listen carefully. If you don't understand anything, tell me, okay?

**Simpson:** All right.

**Vannatter:** Okay, Mr. Simpson, you have the right to remain silent. If you give up the right to remain silent, anything you say can and will be used in a court of law. You have the right to speak with an attorney and to have an attorney during the questioning. If you so desire and cannot afford one, an attorney will be appointed for you without charge before questioning. Do you understand your rights?

**Simpson:** Yes I do.

**Vannatter:** Are there any questions about that?

**Simpson:** [Unintelligible]

**Vannatter:** Okay, you've got to speak louder than that.

**Simpson:** Okay, no.

**Vannatter:** Okay, do you wish to give up your right to remain silent and talk to us?

**Simpson:** Ah, yes.

**Vannatter:** Okay, and you give up your right to have an attorney present while we talk?

**Simpson:** Mmm-hmm. Yes.

**Vannatter:** Okay. All right, what we're gonna do is, we want to, we're investigating, obviously, the death of your ex-wife and another man.

**Simpson:** Someone told us that.

**Vannatter:** Yeah, and we're going to need to talk to you about that. Are you divorced from her now?

**Simpson:** Yes.

**Vannatter:** How long have you been divorced?

**Simpson:** Officially? Probably close to two years, but we've been apart for a little over two years.

**Vannatter:** Have you?

**Simpson:** Yeah.

**Vannatter:** What was your relationship with her? What was the . . .

**Simpson:** Well, we tried to get back together, and it just didn't work—it wasn't working. So we both were going our separate ways.

**Vannatter:** Recently you tried to get back together?

**Simpson:** We tried to get back together for about a year, you know, where we started dating each other and seeing each other. She came back and wanted us to get back together, and . . .

**Vannatter:** Within the last year, you're talking about?

**Simpson:** She came back about a year and four months ago about us trying to get back together, and we gave it a shot. We gave it a shot the better part of a year. And I think we both knew it wasn't working, and probably three weeks ago or so we said it just wasn't working, and we went our separate ways.

**Vannatter:** Okay, the two children are yours?

**Simpson:** Yes.

**Lange:** She have custody?

**Simpson:** We have joint custody.

**Lange:** Through the courts?

**Simpson:** We went through the courts and everything. Everything is done. We have no problems with the kids, we do things together, you know, with the kids.

**Vannatter:** How was your separation? Was that a . . .

**Simpson:** The first separation?

**Vannatter:** Yeah, was there problems with that?

**Simpson:** For me, it was big problems. I loved her, I didn't want us to separate.

**Vannatter:** Uh-huh. I understand that she had made a couple of crime . . . crime reports or something?

**Simpson:** Ah, we had a big fight about six years ago on New Year's, you know, she made a report. I didn't make a report. And then we had an altercation about a year ago maybe. It wasn't a physical argument. I kicked her door or something.

**Vannatter:** And she made a police report on those two occasions?

**Simpson:** Mmm-hmm. And I stayed right there until the police came, talked to them.

**Lange:** Were you arrested at one time for something?

**Simpson:** No. I mean, five years ago we had a big fight, six years ago, I don't know. I know I ended up doing community service.

**Vannatter:** So you weren't arrested?

**Simpson:** No, I was never really arrested.

**Lange:** They never booked you in?

**Simpson:** No.

**Vannatter:** Can I ask you, when's the last time you've slept?

**Simpson:** I got a couple of hours' sleep last night. I mean, you know, I slept a little on the plane, not much, and when I got to the hotel I was asleep a few hours when the phone call came.

**Lange:** Did Nicole have a housemaid that lived there?

**Simpson:** I believe so, yes.

**Lange:** Do you know her name at all?

**Simpson:** Avia . . . Alvia, something like that.

**Vannatter:** We didn't see her there. Did she have the day off, perhaps?

**Simpson:** I don't know. I don't know what schedule she's on.

**Lange:** Phil, what do you think? We can maybe just re-count last night.

**Vannatter:** Yeah. When was the last time you saw Nicole?

**Simpson:** We were leaving a dance recital. She took off and I was talking to her parents.

**Vannatter:** Where was the dance recital?

**Simpson:** Paul Revere High School.

**Vannatter:** And was that for one of your children?

**Simpson:** For my daughter Sydney.

**Vannatter:** And what time was that yesterday?

**Simpson:** It ended about six-thirty, quarter to seven, something like that, you know in the ballpark, right in that area. And they took off.

**Vannatter:** They?

**Simpson:** Her and her family, her mother and father, sisters, my kids, you know.

**Vannatter:** And then you went your own separate ways?

**Simpson:** Yeah, actually she left, and then came back and her mother got in a car with her, and the kids all piled into her sister's car, and they . . .

**Vannatter:** Was Nicole driving?

**Simpson:** Yeah.

**Vannatter:** What kind of car was she driving?

**Simpson:** Her black car, a Cherokee, a Jeep Cherokee.

**Vannatter:** What were you driving?

**Simpson:** My Rolls-Royce . . . my Bentley, rather.

**Vannatter:** Do you own that Ford Bronco that sits outside?

**Simpson:** Hertz owns it and Hertz lets me use it.

**Vannatter:** So that's your vehicle, the one that was parked there on the street?

**Simpson:** Mmm-hmm.

**Vannatter:** And it's actually owned by Hertz?

**Simpson:** Hertz, yeah.

**Vannatter:** Who's the primary driver on that? You?

**Simpson:** I drive it, the housekeeper drives it, you know, it's kind of a . . .

**Vannatter:** All-purpose type vehicle?

**Simpson:** Yeah—it's the only one that my insurance will allow me to let anyone else drive.

**Vannatter:** Okay.

**Lange:** When you drive it, where do you park it at home?

**Simpson:** It depends . . .

**Lange:** Where it is now, it was in the street or something?

**Simpson:** I always park it on the street.

**Lange:** You never take it in the . . .

**Simpson:** Oh, rarely. I mean, I'll bring it in and switch the stuff, you know, and stuff like that. I did that yesterday, you know.

**Lange:** When did you last drive it?

**Simpson:** Yesterday.

**Vannatter:** What time yesterday?

**Simpson:** In the morning, in the afternoon.

**Vannatter:** Okay, you left her, you're saying, about six-thirty or seven, or she left the recital?

**Simpson:** Yeah.

**Vannatter:** And you spoke with her parents?

**Simpson:** Yeah, we were just sitting there talking.

**Vannatter:** What time did you leave the recital?

**Simpson:** Right about that time. We were all leaving. We were all leaving then. Her mother said something about me joining them for dinner and I said no thanks.

**Vannatter:** Where did you go from there, O.J.?

**Simpson:** Ah, home, home for a while, got my car for a while, tried to find my girlfriend for a while, came back to the house.

**Vannatter:** Who was home when you got home?

**Simpson:** Kato.

**Vannatter:** Kato? Anybody else? Was your daughter there, Arnelle?

**Simpson:** No.

**Vannatter:** Isn't that her name, Arnelle?

**Simpson:** Arnelle, yeah.

**Vannatter:** So what time do you think you got back home, actually physically got home?

**Simpson:** Seven-something.

**Vannatter:** Seven-something? And then you left, and . . .

**Simpson:** Yeah, I'm trying to think, did I leave? You know I'm always . . . I had to run and get my daughter some flowers. I was actually doing the recital, so I rushed and got her some flowers, and I came home, and then I called Paula as I was going to her house, and Paula wasn't home.

**Vannatter:** Paula is your girlfriend?

**Simpson:** Girlfriend, yeah.

**Vannatter:** Paula who?

**Simpson:** Barbieri.

**Vannatter:** Could you spell that for me?

**Simpson:** B-A-R-B-I-E-R-I.

**Vannatter:** Do you know an address on her?

**Simpson:** No, she lives on Wilshire, but I think she's out of town.

**Vannatter:** You got a phone number?

**Simpson:** Yeah, of course . . . [telephone number redacted].

**Vannatter:** So you didn't see her last night?

**Simpson:** No, we'd been to a big affair the night before, and then I came back home. I was basically at home. I mean, anytime I was . . . whatever time it took me to get to the recital and back, to get to the flower shop and back, I mean, that's the time I was out of the house.

**Vannatter:** Were you scheduled to play golf this morning, someplace?

**Simpson:** In Chicago.

**Vannatter:** What kind of a tournament was it?

**Simpson:** Ah, it was Hertz, with special clients.

**Vannatter:** Oh, okay. What time did you leave last night, leave the house?

**Simpson:** To go to the airport?

**Vannatter:** Mmm-hmm.

**Simpson:** About . . . the limo was supposed to be there at ten-forty-five. Normally, they get there a little earlier. I was rushing around, somewhere between there and eleven o'clock.

**Vannatter:** So approximately ten-forty-five to eleven?

**Simpson:** Eleven o'clock, yeah, somewhere in that area.

**Vannatter:** And you went by limo?

**Simpson:** Yeah.

**Vannatter:** Who's the limo service?

**Simpson:** Ah, you'd have to ask my office.

**Lange:** Did you converse with the driver at all? Did you talk to him?

**Simpson:** No, he was a new driver. Normally, I have a regular driver I drive with and converse. No, just about rushing to the airport, about how I live my life on airplanes, and hotels, that type of thing.

**Lange:** What time did your plane leave?

**Simpson:** Ah, eleven-forty-five the flight took off.

**Vannatter:** What airline was it?

**Simpson:** American.

**Vannatter:** American? And it was eleven-forty-five to Chicago?

**Simpson:** Chicago.

**Lange:** So yesterday you did drive the white Bronco?

**Simpson:** Mmm-hmm.

**Lange:** And where did you park it when you brought it home?

**Simpson:** Ah, the first time probably by the mailbox. I'm trying to think, or did I bring it in the driveway? Normally, I will park it by the mailbox, sometimes . . .

**Lange:** On Ashford, or Ashland?

**Simpson:** On Ashford, yeah.

**Lange:** Where did you park yesterday for the last time, do you remember?

**Simpson:** Right where it is.

**Lange:** Where is it now?

**Simpson:** Yeah.

**Lange:** Where, on . . .

**Simpson:** Right on the street there.

**Lange:** On Ashford?

**Simpson:** No, on Rockingham.

**Lange:** You parked it there?

**Simpson:** Yes.

**Lange:** About what time was that?

**Simpson:** Eight-something, seven . . . eight, nine o'clock, I don't know, right in that area.

**Lange:** Did you take it to the recital?

**Simpson:** No.

**Lange:** What time was the recital?

**Simpson:** Over at about six-thirty. Like I said, I came home, I got my car, I was going to see my girlfriend. I was calling her, and she wasn't around.

**Lange:** So you drive the, you came home in the Rolls, and then you got in the Bronco?

**Simpson:** In the Bronco 'cause my phone was in the Bronco. And because it's a Bronco. It's a Bronco, it's what I drive, you know. I'd rather drive it than any other car. And, you know, as I was going over there I called her a couple of times, and she wasn't there, and I left a message, and then I checked my messages, and there were no messages. She wasn't there, and she may have to leave town. Then I came back and ended up sitting with Kato.

**Lange:** Okay. What time was this again that you parked the Bronco?

**Simpson:** Eight-something, maybe. He hadn't done a Jacuzzi, we had . . . went and got a burger, and I'd come home and kind of leisurely got ready to go. I mean we'd done a few things.

**Lange:** You weren't in a hurry when you came back with the Bronco?

**Simpson:** No.

**Lange:** The reason I ask you, the car was parked kind of at a funny angle, stuck out in the street.

**Simpson:** Well, it's parked because . . . I don't know if it's a funny angle or what. It's parked because when I was hustling at the end of the day to get all my stuff, and I was getting my phone and everything off it, when I just pulled it out of the gate there, it's like, it's a tight turn.

**Lange:** So you had it inside the compound, then?

**Simpson:** Yeah.

**Lange:** Oh, okay.

**Simpson:** I brought it inside the compound to get my stuff out of it, and then I put it out, and I'd run back inside the gate before the gate closed.

**Vannatter:** How did you get the injury on your hand?

**Simpson:** I don't know. The first time, when I was in Chicago and all, but at the house I was just running around.

**Vannatter:** How did you do it in Chicago?

**Simpson:** I broke a glass. One of you guys had just called me, and I was in the bathroom, and I just kind of went bonkers for a little bit.

**Lange:** Is that how you cut it?

**Simpson:** Mmm, it was cut before, but I think I just opened it again, I'm not sure.

**Lange:** Do you recall bleeding at all in your truck, in the Bronco?

**Simpson:** I recall bleeding at my house, and then I went to the Bronco. The last thing I did before I left, when I was rushing, was went and got my phone out of the Bronco.

**Lange:** Mmm-hmm. Where's the phone now?

**Simpson:** In my bag.

**Lange:** You have it?

**Simpson:** In that black bag.

**Lange:** You brought a bag with you here?

**Simpson:** Yeah.

**Lange:** Do you recall bleeding at all?

**Simpson:** Yeah, I mean, I know I was bleeding, but it was no big deal. I bleed all the time. I play golf and stuff, so there's always something, nicks and stuff, here and there.

**Lange:** So did you do something? When did you put the Band-Aid on it?

**Simpson:** Actually, I asked the girl this morning for it.

**Lange:** And she got it?

**Simpson:** Yeah, 'cause last night with Kato, when I was leaving, he was saying something to me, and I was rushing to get my phone, and I put a little thing on it, and it stopped.

**Vannatter:** Do you have the keys to the Bronco?

**Simpson:** Yeah.

**Vannatter:** Okay. We've impounded the Bronco. I don't know if you know that or not.

**Simpson:** No.

**Vannatter:** To take a look at it. Other than you, who's the last person to drive it?

**Simpson:** Probably Gigi. When I'm out of town, I don't know who drives the car, maybe my daughter, maybe Kato.

**Vannatter:** The keys are available?

**Simpson:** I leave the keys there, you know, when Gigi's there, because sometimes she needs it, or Gigi was off and wasn't coming back until today, and I was coming back tonight.

**Vannatter:** So you don't mind if Gigi uses it, or . . .

**Simpson:** This is the only one I can let her use. When she doesn't have her car, 'cause sometimes her husband takes her car, I let her use the car.

**Lange:** When was the last time you were at Nicole's house?

**Simpson:** I don't go in, I don't go in her house. I haven't been in her house in a week, maybe five days. I go to her house a lot. I mean, I'm always dropping the kids off, picking the kids up, fooling around with the dog, you know.

**Vannatter:** How does that usually work? Do you drop them at the porch, or do you go in with them?

**Simpson:** No, I don't go in the house.

**Vannatter:** Is there a kind of gate out front?

**Simpson:** Yeah.

**Vannatter:** But you never go inside the house?

**Simpson:** Up until five days, six days ago, I haven't been in the house. Once I started seeing Paula again, I kind of avoid Nicole.

**Vannatter:** Is Nicole seeing anybody else that you . . .

**Simpson:** I have no idea. I really have absolutely no idea. I don't ask her, I don't know. Her and her girlfriends, they go out, you know, they've got some things going on right now with her girlfriends, so I'm assuming something's happening because one of her girlfriends is having a big problem with her husband because she's always saying she's with Nicole until three or four in the morning. She's not. You know, Nicole tells me she leaves here at one-thirty or two or two-thirty, and the girl doesn't get home until five, and she only lives a few blocks away.

**Vannatter:** Something's going on, huh?

**Lange:** Do you know where they went, the family, for dinner last night?

**Simpson:** No. Well, no, I didn't ask.

**Lange:** I just thought maybe there's a regular place they go.

**Simpson:** No. If I was with them, we'd go to Toscano [Toscana]. I mean, not Toscano, Poponi's [Peppone].

**Vannatter:** You haven't had any problems with her lately, have you, O.J.?

**Simpson:** I always have problems with her, you know. Our relationship has been a problem relationship. Probably lately for me, and I say this only because I said it to Ron yesterday at the—Ron Fishman, whose wife is Cora—at the dance recital, when he came up to me and went "Oooh, boy, what's going on?" And everybody was beefing with everybody, and I said, "Well I'm just glad I'm out of the mix." You know, because I was like dealing with him and his problems with his wife and Nicole and evidently some new problems that a guy named Christian was having with his girl and was staying at Nicole's house, and something was going on, but I don't think it's pertinent to this.

**Vannatter:** Did Nicole have words with you last night?

**Simpson:** Pardon me?

**Vannatter:** Did Nicole have words with you last night?

**Simpson:** No, not at all.

**Vannatter:** Did you talk to her last night?

**Simpson:** To ask to speak to my daughter, to congratulate my daughter, and everything.

**Vannatter:** But you didn't have a conversation with her?

**Simpson:** No, no.

**Vannatter:** What were you wearing last night, O.J.?

**Simpson:** What I wore, I wore on the golf course yesterday, some of these kind of pants, some of these kind of pants, I mean I changed different for the whatever it was. I just had on some . . .

**Vannatter:** Just these black pants.

**Simpson:** Just these . . . they're called Bugle Boy.

**Vannatter:** Bugle Boy? Is that what you wore to the recital?

**Simpson:** No, to the recital I wore . . . what did I wear to the recital? I wore a white T-shirt and some slacks.

**Vannatter:** These aren't the pants?

**Simpson:** No.

**Vannatter:** Where are the pants that you wore?

**Simpson:** They're hanging in my closet.

**Vannatter:** These are washable, right? You just throw them in the laundry?

**Simpson:** Yeah, I got a hundred pair. They give them to me free, Bugle Boy, so I've got a bunch of them.

**Vannatter:** Do you recall coming home and hanging them up, or . . .

**Simpson:** I always hang up my clothes. I mean it's rare that I don't hang up my clothes unless I'm laying them in my bathroom for her to do something with them. But those are the only things I don't hang up. But when you play golf you don't necessarily dirty pants.

**Lange:** What kind of shoes were you wearing?

**Simpson:** Tennis shoes.

**Lange:** Tennis shoes? Do you know what kind?

**Simpson:** Probably Reebok, that's all I wear.

**Lange:** Are they at home, too?

**Simpson:** Yeah.

**Lange:** Was this just to be a short trip to Chicago, so you didn't take a whole lot?

**Simpson:** Yeah, I was coming back today.

**Lange:** Just overnight?

**Simpson:** Yeah.

**Vannatter:** That's a hectic schedule, drive back here to play golf and come back.

**Simpson:** Yeah, but I do it all the time.

**Vannatter:** Do you?

**Simpson:** Yeah. That's what I was complaining with the driver about, you know, about my whole life is on and off airplanes.

**Vannatter:** O.J., we've got sort of a problem.

**Simpson:** Mmm-hmm.

**Vannatter:** We've got some blood on and in your car, we've got some blood at your house, and it's sort of a problem.

**Simpson:** Well, take my blood—test it.

**Lange:** Well, we'd like to do that. We've got, of course the cut on your finger that you aren't real clear on. Do you recall having that cut on your finger the last time you were at Nicole's house?

**Simpson:** [Pause] A week ago?

**Lange:** Yeah.

**Simpson:** No, it was last night.

**Lange:** Okay, so it was last night you cut it?

**Vannatter:** Somewhere after the recital?

**Simpson:** Somewhere when I was rushing to get out of my house.

**Vannatter:** Okay, after the recital?

**Simpson:** Yeah.

**Vannatter:** What do you think happened? Do you have any idea?

**Simpson:** I have no idea, man. You guys haven't told me anything. I have no idea what happened. When you said to my daughter, who said something to me today, that somebody else might have been involved. I have absolutely no idea what happened. I don't know how, why, or what. I mean, you guys haven't told me anything. Every time I ask you guys, you say you're going to tell me in a bit.

**Vannatter:** Well, we don't know a lot of the answers to these questions yet ourselves, O.J., okay?

**Simpson:** I've got a bunch of guns, guns all over the place. You can take them, they're all there, I mean, you can see them. I keep them in my car for an incident that happened a month ago that my in-laws, my wife and everybody knows about that.

**Vannatter:** What was that?

**Simpson:** Going down to . . . and cops down there know about it because I've told two marshals about it at a mall. I was going down for a christening, and I had just left our set and it was like three-thirty in the morning and I am in a lane, and all of a sudden the car in front of me is going real slow, and I'm slowing down 'cause I figure he sees a cop, 'cause we were all going pretty fast and I'm going to change lanes, but there's a car next to me and I can't change lanes. Then that goes for a while, and I'm going to slow down and go around him, but the car butts up to me and I'm like caught between three cars. They were Oriental guys, and they were not letting me go anywhere. And finally I went on the shoulder, and I sped up, and then I held my phone up so they could see the light part of it, you know, 'cause I have tinted the windows, and they kind of scattered, and I chased one of them for a while to make him think I was chasing him before I took off.

**Lange:** Were you in the Bronco?

**Simpson:** No.

**Lange:** What were you driving?

**Simpson:** My Bentley. It has tinted windows and all, so I figured they thought they had a nice little touch.

**Lange:** Did you think they were trying to rip you off?

**Simpson:** Definitely, they were. And then the next day, you know, Nicole and I, I went home. At four in the morning I got there to Laguna, and when we woke up, I told her about it, and told her parents about it, told everybody about it, you know? And when I saw two marshals at a mall, I walked up and told them about it.

**Vannatter:** What did they do, make a report on it?

**Simpson:** They didn't know nothing. I mean, they'll remember me and remember I told them.

**Vannatter:** Did Nicole mention that she'd been getting any threats lately to you? Anything she was concerned about or the kids' safety?

**Simpson:** To her?

**Vannatter:** Yes.

**Simpson:** From?

**Vannatter:** From anybody?

**Simpson:** No, not at all.

**Vannatter:** Was she very security-conscious? Did she keep that house locked up?

**Simpson:** Very.

**Vannatter:** The intercom didn't work apparently, right?

**Simpson:** I thought it worked.

**Vannatter:** Oh, okay. Does the electronic buzzer work?

**Simpson:** The electronic buzzer works to let people in.

**Vannatter:** Do you ever park in the rear when you go over there?

**Simpson:** Most of the time.

**Vannatter:** You do park in the rear?

**Simpson:** Most times when I'm taking the kids there, I come right into the driveway, blow the horn, and she, or a lot of times the housekeeper, either the housekeeper opens or they'll keep a garage door open up on the top of the thing, you know, but that's when I'm dropping the kids off, and I'm not going in, and sometimes I go to the front because the kids have to hit the buzzer and stuff.

**Vannatter:** Did you say before that up until about three weeks ago you guys were going out again and trying to . . .

**Simpson:** No, we'd been going out for about a year, and then the last six months it hadn't been working so we tried various things to see if we could make it work. We started trying to date and that wasn't working, and so, you know, we just said the hell with it, you know.

**Vannatter:** And that was about three weeks ago?

**Simpson:** Yeah, about three weeks ago.

**Vannatter:** So were you seeing her up to that point?

**Simpson:** It's, to say I was seeing her, yeah, I mean yeah, yeah it was a done deal, it just wasn't happening. I mean, I was gone. I mean, I was in San Juan doing a film, and I don't think we had sex since I've been back from San Juan, and that was like two months ago. So it's been like . . . for the kids we tried to do things together. We didn't go out together, you know, we didn't really date each other. Then we decided let's try to date each other. We went out one night, and it just didn't work.

**Vannatter:** When you say it didn't work, what do you mean?

**Simpson:** Ah, the night we went out it was fun. Then the next night we went out it was actually when I was down in Laguna, and she didn't want to go out. And I said, "Well, let's go out 'cause I came all the way down here to go out," and we kind of had a beef. And it just didn't work after that, you know? We were only trying to date to see if we could bring romance back into our relationship. We just said, let's treat each other like boyfriend and girlfriend instead of, you know, like seventeen-year-old married people. I mean, seventeen years together, whatever that is.

**Vannatter:** How long were you together?

**Simpson:** Seventeen years.

**Vannatter:** Seventeen years. Did you ever hit her, O.J.?

**Simpson:** Ah, one night we had a fight. We had a fight and she hit me. And they never took my statement, they never wanted to hear my side and they never wanted to hear the housekeeper's side. Nicole was drunk. She did her thing, she started tearing up my house, you know? And I didn't punch her or anything, but I . . .

**Vannatter:** Slapped her a couple of times?

**Simpson:** No, no I wrestled her, is what I did. I didn't slap her at all. I mean, Nicole's a strong girl. She's a . . . one of the most conditioned women. Since that period of time, she's hit me a few times, but I've never touched her after that and I'm telling you, it's five, six years ago.

**Vannatter:** What's her birthday?

**Simpson:** May 19th.

**Vannatter:** Did you get together with her on her birthday?

**Simpson:** Yeah, her and I and the kids, I believe.

**Vannatter:** Did you give her a gift?

**Simpson:** I gave her a gift.

**Vannatter:** What'd you give her?

**Simpson:** I gave her either a bracelet or the earrings.

**Vannatter:** Did she keep them or . . .

**Simpson:** Oh, no, when we split she gave me both the earrings and the bracelet back. I bought her a very nice bracelet, I didn't know if it was Mother's Day or her birthday, and I bought her the earrings for the other thing, and when we split, and it's a credit to her, she felt that it wasn't right that she had it, and I said good, because I want them back.

**Vannatter:** Was that the very day of her birthday, May 19th, or was it a few days later?

**Simpson:** What do you mean?

**Vannatter:** You gave it to her on the 19th of May, her birthday, right, this bracelet?

**Simpson:** I may have given her the earrings. No, the bracelet. May 19th. When was Mother's Day?

**Vannatter:** Mother's Day was around that . . .

**Simpson:** No, it was probably her birthday, yes.

**Vannatter:** And did she return it the same day?

**Simpson:** Oh, no, she . . . I'm in a funny place here on this, all right? She returned it—both of them—maybe three weeks ago or so. When I say I'm in a funny place on this, I gave it to my girlfriend and told her I bought it for her, you know? That was three weeks ago. I told her I bought it for her. What am I going to do with it?

**Lange:** Did Mr. Weitzman, your attorney, talk to you anything about this polygraph we brought up before? What are your thoughts on that?

**Simpson:** Should I talk about my thoughts on that?

**Lange:** It's up to you.

**Simpson:** I'm sure eventually I'll do it, but it's like I've got some weird thoughts now. I've had weird thoughts . . . you know when you've been with a person for seventeen years, you think everything. I've got to understand what this thing is. If it's true blue, I don't mind doing it.

**Lange:** Well, you're not compelled at all to take this, number one, and number two, I don't know if Mr. Weitzman explained it to you—this goes to the exclusion of someone as much as to the inclusion so we can eliminate people. And just to get things straight . . .

**Simpson:** But does it work for elimination?

**Lange:** Oh, yes. We use it for elimination more than anything.

**Simpson:** Well, I'll talk to him about it.

**Lange:** Understand, the reason we're talking to you is because you're the ex-husband.

**Simpson:** I know I'm the number one target, and now you tell me I've got blood all over the place.

**Lange:** Well, there's blood in your house and in the driveway, and we've got a search warrant, and we're going to get the blood. We found some in your house. Is that your blood that's there?

**Simpson:** If it's dripped, it's what I dripped running around trying to leave.

**Lange:** Last night?

**Simpson:** Yeah, and I wasn't aware that it was . . . I was aware that I . . . you know I was trying to get out of the house, I didn't even pay any attention to it. I saw it when I was in the kitchen, and I grabbed a napkin or something, and that was it. I didn't think about it after that.

**Vannatter:** That was last night after you got home from the recital, when you were rushing?

**Simpson:** That was last night when I was . . . I don't know what I was, I was in the car getting my junk out of the car. I was in the house throwing hangers and stuff in my suitcase. I was doing my little crazy what I do, I mean, I do it everywhere. Anybody who has ever picked me up says that O.J.'s a whirlwind. He's running, he's grabbing things, and that's what I was doing.

**Vannatter:** Well, I'm going to step out and I'm going to get a photographer to come down and photograph your hand there. And then here pretty soon we're going to take you downstairs and get some blood from you. Okay? I'll be right back.

**Lange:** So it was about five days ago you last saw Nicole? Was it at the house?

**Simpson:** Okay, the last time I saw Nicole, physically saw Nicole, I saw her obviously last night. The time before,

I'm trying to think. I went to Washington, D.C., so I didn't see her, so I'm trying to think. I haven't seen her since I went to Washington. I went to Washington— what's the day today?

**Lange:** Today's Monday, the 13th of June.

**Simpson:** Okay, I went to Washington on maybe Wednesday. Thursday, I think I was in . . . Thursday I was in Connecticut, then Long Island Thursday afternoon and all of Friday. I got home Friday night, Friday afternoon, I played, you know . . . Paula picked me up at the airport. I played golf Saturday, and when I came home I think my son was there. So I did something with my son. I don't think I saw Nicole at all then. And then I went to a big affair with Paula Saturday night, and I got up and played golf Sunday, which pissed Paula off, and I saw Nicole at . . . it was about a week before, I saw her at the . . .

**Lange:** Okay, the last time you saw Nicole, was that at her house?

**Simpson:** I don't remember. I wasn't in her house, so it couldn't have been at her house, so it was, you know, I don't physically remember the last time I saw her. I may have seen her even jogging one day.

**Lange:** Let me get this straight. You've never physically been inside the house?

**Simpson:** Not in the last week.

**Lange:** Ever. I mean, how long has she lived there? About six months?

**Simpson:** Oh, Christ, I've slept at that house many, many, many times, you know? I've done everything at that house, you know? I'm just saying . . . you're talking in the week or so.

**Lange:** Well, whatever. Six months she's lived there?

**Simpson:** I don't know. Roughly. I was at her house maybe two weeks ago, ten days ago. One night her and I had a long talk, you know, about how can we make it better for the kids, and I told her we'd do things better. And, okay, I can almost say when that was. That was when I, I don't know, it was about ten days ago. And then we . . . the next day I had her leave her dog, do a flea bath or something with me. Oh, I'll tell you, I did see her one day I went . . . I don't know if this was the early part of last week, I went 'cause my son had to go get something, and he ran in, and she came to the gate, and the dog ran out, and her friend Faye and I went looking for the dog. That may have been a week ago, I don't know.

**Lange (to Vannatter):** Got a photographer coming?

**Vannatter:** No, we're going to take him up there.

**Lange:** We're ready to terminate this at 14:07.

# GLOSSARY

||||||||||||||||||||

**Anchoring** – A term used in the negotiation context to describe a person's heavy reliance on the first piece of information provided or offer made by the other party, creating an expectation of an outcome other than what was first envisaged.

**Anchor point** – Any part of the body that anchors a person to a particular spot or position, including the feet, which are always anchor points. We look at anchor point movement as a potential nonverbal deceptive behavior in which anxiety is dissipated through the physical movement.

**Attack behavior** – A verbal deceptive behavior in which a person attacks the questioner as a means of compelling him to back off from a particular line of questioning. This often takes the form of attempting to impeach the credibility or competence of the questioner. Example: "How long have you been doing this job?"

**Autonomic nervous system** – The part of the nervous system that controls the functions of body organs and involuntary physical reactions to stimuli.

**Bait question** – A question that establishes a hypothetical situation and is designed to trigger a mind virus. Bait questions typically begin with the phrase, "Is there any reason that . . ."

**Baselining** – Comparing observed behavior with an established norm. This is a behavior assessment strategy that we recommend be avoided because of the high potential for drawing a faulty conclusion.

**Behavioral pause/delay** – A nonverbal deceptive behavior in which a silent gap precedes a person's response to a question.

**Catch-all question** – A wrap-up question that is designed to uncover lies of omission, and to serve as a safety net in the event that the questioner inadvertently overlooks an issue. Example: "What haven't we discussed that's important for me to know about?"

**Cliff moment** – The arrival at a point when a person feels he has disclosed everything he is able to disclose without suffering negative consequences. To go further would be tantamount to "jumping off the cliff."

**Close-ended question** – A question that's used to probe specific case facts. Example: "Who was already in the office when you arrived this morning?"

**Cluster** – Any combination of two or more deceptive indicators.

**Cognitive dissonance** – A cognitive bias in which a person feels discomfort as a result of holding two contradictory views.

**Commitment/consistency** – A term coined by social psychologist Robert Cialdini to describe the compelling desire of people to act in accordance with a position they have previously taken, or a commitment they have previously made.

**Compound question** – A question type that is to be avoided because it contains more than one question, making behavioral analysis of the response difficult due to potential confusion over what part of the question is causing the deceptive behavior. Example: "How frequently do you go running, and where do you typically run?"

**Confirmation bias** – A cognitive bias in which people search for or interpret information in a way that supports an initial belief or a desired outcome.

**Convincing statement** – A true or irrefutable statement made in an effort to convince the accuser and to influence his perception, rather than to convey information that addresses the facts of the case.

**Denial behavior** – A category of verbal deceptive behavior in which a person appears to have a problem with denying an allegation. This can take the form of failing to deny the allegation altogether; providing a nonspecific denial (Example: "I would never do something like that"); or providing an isolated delivery of the denial by burying it in a long-winded answer.

**Direct observation of concern (DOC)** – A transition statement that lies at the low end of the confidence spectrum.

**Direct observation of guilt (DOG)** – A transition statement that lies at the high end of the confidence spectrum.

**Elicitation** – A process designed to influence or persuade an individual to reveal information that he has reason to want to conceal. This process is characterized by use of a monologue rather than a dialogue. (Used synonymously with *interrogation*.)

**Equitable distribution** – A term used to describe the legal process of dividing a married couple's assets in a divorce proceeding.

**Exclusion qualifier** – A verbal deceptive behavior used to enable a person who wants to withhold certain information to answer a question truthfully, but without releasing that information. Examples: "basically," "for the most part," "fundamentally," "probably," "most often."

**Failure to answer** – A verbal deceptive behavior in which a person's response does not answer the question that's asked.

**Failure to understand a simple question** – A verbal deceptive behavior in which a person's response is an expression of confusion over an easily comprehensible question. This strategy is typically used when a person feels trapped by the wording of the question and needs to shrink its scope.

**Fight-or-flight response** – A triggering of the autonomic nervous system that reroutes circulation to the body's major organs and muscle groups to prepare the body to deal with a threatening situation.

**Forer effect** – A cognitive bias named for psychologist Bertram Forer, who found that people tend to rate as highly accurate a personality analysis that is presented as being individualized, when it is actually so general in nature that it could apply to almost anyone. (Also known as Barnum statements.)

**Global behavior assessment** – A behavior assessment strategy that focuses on maximizing information collection and analyzing general behavior, rather than focusing on specific behaviors exhibited in response to a question.

**Grooming gesture** – A nonverbal deceptive behavior in which anxiety is dissipated through physical activity in the form of grooming oneself or the immediate surroundings.

**Halo effect** – A cognitive bias in which a person is viewed favorably on the basis of a single positive attribute or impression.

**Hand-to-face activity** – A nonverbal deceptive behavior in which a person touches his face or head region in response to a question, which can be prompted by discomfort associated with circulatory changes triggered by the fight-or-flight response.

**Hiding mouth or eyes** – A nonverbal deceptive behavior in which a person uses a hand to shield his mouth or eyes when responding to a question, or closes his eyes when responding to a question that does not require reflection.

**Ideational fluency** – The ability to shift one's thinking instantaneously as the situation warrants.

**Inappropriate level of concern** – A verbal deceptive behavior in which a person attempts to equalize the exchange by trying to diminish the importance of the matter at hand. He may focus on either the issue or the process (Example: "Why is everybody making such a big deal about this?"); or he might even attempt to joke about it.

**Inappropriate level of politeness** – A verbal deceptive behavior in which a person interjects an overly polite or unexpectedly kind or complimentary comment directed at the questioner when responding to a question. Example: Uncharacteristic use of "sir" or "ma'am" when responding to a particular question.

**Inappropriate question** – A verbal deceptive behavior in which a person responds with a question that doesn't directly relate to the question that's asked.

**Inconsistent statement** – A verbal deceptive behavior in which a person makes a statement that is inconsistent with what he said previously, without explaining why the story has changed.

**Interrogation** – See *Elicitation*.

**Interview** – A means of establishing a dialogue with a person to collect information that he has no reason to want to withhold.

**Invoking religion** – A verbal deceptive behavior in which a person makes a reference to God or religion as a means of "dressing up the lie" before presenting it. Example: "I swear on a stack of Bibles, I wouldn't do anything like that."

**Leading question** – A question that contains the answer that the questioner is looking for.

**Legitimacy statement** – A statement within a monologue that is designed to explain the purpose or reasoning behind what the interrogator is conveying.

**Lie of commission** – A lie that is conveyed by means of making a statement that is untrue.

**Lie of influence** – A lie that is conveyed by means of attempting to manipulate perception rather than to provide truthful information.

**Lie of omission** – A lie that is conveyed by means of withholding the truth.

**L-squared mode** – Using one's visual and auditory senses to *look* and *listen* simultaneously in order to observe both verbal and nonverbal deceptive behaviors as they're exhibited in response to a question.

**Microexpression** – A split-second movement of facial muscles that conveys an emotion such as anger, contempt, or disgust. We recommend avoiding reliance on microexpressions, due to their impracticality and the fact that there is no microexpression for deception.

**Mind virus** – A colloquial term for the psychological discomfort a person feels when he receives information that has potentially negative consequences, causing his mind to race with hypothetical ramifications of the information.

**Minimization** – An element within a monologue that is designed to minimize the perception of negative consequences that may be associated with sharing truthful information.

**Mirroring** – Subtly imitating the movements or gestures of another person to enhance familiarity and liking.

**Monologue** – A verbal exercise that characterizes the elicitation process, designed to keep the person in short-term thinking mode, dissuade him from expressing resistance or voicing a denial, and convince him of the acceptability of disclosing the information he had intended to withhold.

**Negative question** – A question that is phrased in a way that negates an action. This question type is to be avoided because it conveys an expectation of a response that potentially lets the person off the hook. Example: "You didn't flirt with her, did you?"

**Nonanswer statement** – A verbal deceptive behavior in which a person responds to a question with a statement that does not answer the question, but rather buys him time to formulate a response that he hopes will satisfy the questioner. Example: "That's a very good question."

**Nonverbal deceptive indicator** – A deceptive behavior that is exhibited in response to a question and that does not involve verbal communication.

**Open-ended question** – A question that is asked as a means of establishing the basis for a discussion or to probe an issue. Example: "What were you doing in Las Vegas when you were supposed to be visiting your mother in Tampa?"

**Opinion question** – A question that solicits a person's opinion as a means of assessing his likely culpability in a given situation. The "punishment question" falls into this category. Example: "What do you think should happen to a person who dines in a restaurant and leaves without paying?"

**Optimism bias** – A cognitive bias that causes people to believe that they are less at risk of a negative outcome, or more likely to enjoy a positive outcome, than other people in a given situation.

**Overly specific answer** – A verbal deceptive behavior in which the person's response is too narrow and technical at one extreme, or too detailed and exhaustive at the other.

**Perception qualifier** – A verbal deceptive behavior employed to enhance credibility. Examples: "frankly," "to be perfectly honest," "candidly."

**Presumptive question** – A question that presumes something to be the case.

**Process/procedural complaint** – A verbal deceptive behavior in which a person takes issue with the proceedings. It may be a delaying tactic or an attempt to steer the proceedings down a different path.

**Projection of blame** – An element of a monologue that is designed to encourage a person to share truthful information by suggesting that the blame for the matter at hand does not rest exclusively with him.

**Psychological alibi** – An attempt to deceive through the use of selective memory or ostensibly limited knowledge.

**Psychological entrenchment** – The condition in which a person feels compelled to dig his heels in the ground and stick to his story, making the information collection process especially difficult.

**Question prologue** – A short, narrative explanation preceding a question that is designed to prime the information pump, so that if the person is on the fence about whether or not he's going to give you something, it will help to influence him to come down on your side of the fence.

**Rationalization** – An element of a monologue that is designed to encourage a person to share truthful information by suggesting that there is a socially acceptable reason that to some degree might excuse the activity under investigation.

**Reciprocity** – A term used by social psychologists to describe the tendency of people to respond to a kind act or concession with kindness and conciliation, or, conversely, to an unkind act with comparable unkindness.

**Referral statement** – A verbal deceptive behavior in which a person refers to a previous response to the question. This takes advantage of repetition as a psychological tool that can make the questioner more open to a possibility than he otherwise might have been.

**Reluctance/refusal to answer** – A verbal deceptive behavior in which a person claims to be unable to answer the question, ostensibly due to a lack of knowledge or to being the wrong person to ask.

**Repeating the question** – A verbal deceptive behavior in which a person repeats the question he's asked as a means of buying time to formulate his response.

**Selective memory** – A verbal deceptive behavior in which a person creates a psychological alibi by responding to a question with a stated inability to remember.

**Short-term thinking** – Focusing on what matters at the moment, rather than on potential consequences over the long term.

**Socialization** – An element of a monologue that is designed to encourage a person to share truthful information by suggesting that the activity under investigation is one that is regularly engaged in by others.

**Stimulus** – The question that prompts a behavioral response.

**Throat-clearing/swallowing** – A nonverbal deceptive behavior in which a person clears his throat or performs a significant swallow prior to answering the question.

**Timing** – The guideline in our deception detection model dictating that the initial deceptive behavior must begin within the first five seconds after the stimulus.

**Transition statement** – Statement made by the questioner to allow for a transparent transition from an interview to an interrogation. It is the first sentence or two of the monologue, and takes the form of a direct observation of concern (DOC) or a direct observation of guilt (DOG).

**Unintended message** – A truthful statement made by a deceptive person that, when the literal meaning of the statement is analyzed, conveys information that the person does not realize he's conveying. We also refer to this as "truth in the lie."

**Vague question** – A question to be avoided because it allows for excessive latitude in the response.

**Verbal deceptive indicator** – A deceptive behavior that involves verbal communication in response to a question.

**Verbal/nonverbal disconnect** – A deceptive behavior in which a person's verbal and nonverbal behaviors in response to a question don't match. The most common verbal/nonverbal disconnect occurs when a person nods affirmatively while saying "no," or turns his head from side to side while saying "yes."

# ACKNOWLEDGMENTS

|||||||||||||||||||||||||||||||||||||||||||

At the launch of our previous book, *Spy the Lie*, in the summer of 2012, our agent, Paul Fedorko, came up to us and smiled. "Congratulations," he said. "You know you need to start thinking about the next one, right?"

A master at his craft, Paul foresaw that *Spy the Lie* would be a bestseller, and he was already preparing us for the road that lay ahead. We're deeply grateful to Paul and his team at N.S. Bienstock for giving us that encouraging push out of the gate, and for expertly guiding our steps along the way.

In the acknowledgments we shared in *Spy the Lie*, we noted that throughout the process of writing it, we had been "surrounded by individuals who have demonstrated not only a gracious generosity with their time and expertise, but a genuine desire to help make this book a worthy voice of subject matter that can truly change people's lives for the better." Many of those same individuals, and quite a few others, were equally gracious and generous this time around. Chief among them were our colleagues at our training and consulting company, QVerity, including founding partner Bill Stanton, training specialist Jack Bowden, and marketing guru Bryan Stevenson.

We were extremely fortunate to have an insightful and discerning group of friends, family members, and professional associates who read the manuscript and offered enormously helpful advice on ways to improve it. That perceptive group includes Todd Simkin, Nate Hukill, Bill Fairweather, Dr. Kyle Harner, Lisa Harner, Dr. David Frazier, Vicki Haddock, Spencer Grant, Angela Moss, Bill Ebsworth, Karen Flanagan, Toni Sikes, Richard Johnston, Mike Houston, Casey Houston, Alex Reeves, Stephanie Floyd, Marcy Romary, Dr. Mark Cervi, Dr. Alethia Cook, Dr. Carmine Scavo, Ardith Tennant, Don Tennant II, Dan Tennant, Shelly Tennant, and Alex Wimberly. We also wish to thank Mike Hagel and Dave Kilmer for sharing their artistic expertise by providing valuable feedback on the cover design.

Finally, very special thanks go out to our remarkably talented colleagues at St. Martin's Press. The skilled copy editors and designers, editorial assistants Jaime Coyne and Kate Canfield, and production editor Kenneth J. Silver, worked tirelessly to make this book what we all wanted it to be. Most tireless of all was our editor, Marc Resnick, who couldn't have made this journey any more enjoyable. His editorial vision was keenly incisive, and his ability to balance strong editorial command with an accommodating, gracious style was nothing short of extraordinary.

## PHIL HOUSTON'S PERSONAL ACKNOWLEDGMENTS

*Get the Truth* is a natural outgrowth of our first book, *Spy the Lie*, so it's not surprising that those who helped to make *Spy the Lie* a success are also many of the ones who enabled *Get the Truth* to become a reality. First and foremost, a special thanks to my wife, Debi, for your love and support, and to Phil Jr., Chris, and Beth for making Mom and me so proud of all of you. I'm also very proud and lucky to have a wonderful daughter-in-law, Rebecca, and an equally wonderful son-in-law, Nick Dawson. I want to extend my heartfelt thanks to Phil Jr. and Rebecca, for giving us something even more special than a *New York Times* bestseller. Thanks to them, last October we welcomed our granddaughter, Paige Leigh Houston, to the family.

If not for our agent, Paul Fedorko, and our editor, Marc Resnick, both of our books would still be dreams. Thanks so much, guys! Also, thanks to St. Martin's Press for taking another chance on us.

When a person has partners like Mike Floyd, Susan Carnicero, Don Tennant, and our newcomer, Peter Romary, the ride is fun, meaningful, and most important, one that makes it easy to believe that success is actually within reach.

I cannot forget the original III gang of Jack Bowden, Bill Fairweather, Bill Mitchell, and Gary Baron, who not only are wonderful friends, but are amazing practitioners and teachers of the techniques we write about in both *Spy the Lie* and *Get the Truth*.

Special thanks go out to those at the CIA and those in uniform who continue to fight and sacrifice so that the rest of us sleep easy. Words will never be enough!

I'd also like to mention my siblings: Bill; Mike and his wife, Penny; Casey and his wife, Debbie; and Terri and her husband, Alex. I love you guys dearly, and I know how much we all miss Mom, Dad, and our brother Brett, who passed away unexpectedly last year.

Finally, I would like to make very special mention of my mother-in-law, Frances Winstead; and the biggest *Spy the Lie* fan I know of—my father-in-law, Jim Winstead. He passed away this past year, and I know he's eagerly waiting above to read *Get the Truth*. We miss you!

## MICHAEL FLOYD'S PERSONAL ACKNOWLEDGMENTS

To my darling wife, Estelita, thank you for holding my hand in my quest for the Truth with a capital *T*. To my family, precious friends and colleagues, too numerous to mention by name, please know that I am blessed to have stood on your shoulders. To my dear friend, colleague, and crazy-talented writer of this book, Don Tennant, you have once again worked your magic. Your name may not be in lights, but you will forever shine brightly in my heart. I would also like to express a very special thanks to our loyal QVerity clients for your trust in our ability to serve you.

Lastly, it is with great humility that I acknowledge the strength and fortitude shown by the thousands of men and women who, over the decades, bared their souls to me regarding life-changing missteps—some too grizzly to share, others too minor to matter. Knowing full well your confessions meant certain public scorn, shame, embarrassment, termination, family strain, incarceration, or even potential execution, you still had the courage to stand tall and look your accusers in the eye. For this, I always felt a profound sense of responsibility to gain your trust, and an unwavering resolve to treat you with the dignity, respect, and compassion you deserved. Simply put, when I told you I understood, I did. I never judged you, because I had never walked in your shoes. I always knew, "There but for the grace of God go I."

## SUSAN CARNICERO'S PERSONAL ACKNOWLEDGMENTS

The publication of our second book has afforded me the opportunity to once again reflect on those friends and family members whose support has made this journey of mine successful.

Firstly, my involvement in this project would never have been possible without the unwavering love and support of my wonderful children, Lauren and Nicholas Carnicero. Their understanding and acceptance of my career path have been invaluable, and have allowed me the latitude to do what I do. Fortunately, Lauren and Nick continue on their paths toward young adulthood with grace, kindness and a marvelous wit. No less was expected of them, and I remain immensely proud of both of them.

I would be remiss if I didn't take a moment to also thank my parents, Anna Marie and Jack Brenton, and Cliff Muncy. Your influence and patience throughout my life led me to become the adult I am today, and I thank you for your unconditional love.

And finally, those friends who have supported me without fail throughout many years certainly deserve mention. Unfortunately, I lost one of those dear friends, Sheila Derryberry, to cancer a few months ago. Even when enduring the worst of her illness, she remained a solid support in my life, and an influence that was made even more poignant as I watched her undergo a horrendous and courageous battle for life. Her tenacity and grace in the light of her illness left me awestruck at her strength, and she will be missed immensely. Additionally, Cindy and Steve Gensurowsky remain as close as any family member, and their support in so many areas has been an invaluable part of my life. Cindy has been a continuous sounding board and sanity check (which was certainly needed), and both Cindy and Steve have taken the ride with me through many of my life's ups and downs. More important, they have done so without judgment. And for that, I am eternally grateful.

In retrospect, I am extremely blessed to have all of these people in my life, and I thank them all for the love, direction, and support they have provided me, both in co-authoring this second book, and for being just what I needed, when I needed it.

## PETER ROMARY'S PERSONAL ACKNOWLEDGMENTS

Before I acknowledge those near and dear to me for their kindness, love, and support, I first want to recognize, and commend to readers, those whose work I have studied, absorbed, relied upon, and cited: Dan Ariely, Tali Sharot, Amy Cuddy, Daniel Kahneman, William Ury, and Robert Cialdini. I urge you to read anything you can by these greats.

In my work I have been surrounded by wonderful friends, colleagues, and students—I have learned from each and every one of them. My journey of learning is ongoing, and there are too many people to thank individually, but they know who they are and what they mean to me. That said, I want to recognize and thank my colleagues at Sigma Threat Management Associates, especially Marisa Randazzo, Dorian Van Horn, Andy Patrick, and Gene Deisinger; and I would like to extend a very special thank-you to Jeff Pollard.

I have been supported professionally and personally by my longtime law partner, Jeremy Tanner, and by April Uzzell, the finest paralegal I have ever known. I wish to recognize a few of my colleagues at East Carolina University: Carmine Scavo, Alethia Cook, Brad Lockerbie, and Bob Morphet. I am also eternally grateful to Jim Galloway and Mark Cervi, two of the finest physicians—and friends—I could have ever wished for.

Special thanks also go to my family: to my parents, John and Joy Romary, for their unfailing support and faith in me; and to my in-laws, John and Bobbie Wiggs.

Finally, to my daughter, Elizabeth, and wife, Marcy: You mean everything to me and, while work has taken me away too often, I hope that you always know that I love you deeply, and that I am so very proud of both of you. Without you, my life would be incomplete. The proudest titles I will ever hold are those of father and husband.

## DON TENNANT'S PERSONAL ACKNOWLEDGMENTS

My dad would have loved this book. He used to enjoy reading everything I wrote, but this book would have been special. He met Phil Houston thirty-five years ago, when Phil was a newly recruited CIA officer, and I was finishing my studies at Georgetown University and preparing to join the National Security Agency. As a career military serviceman, he was devoted to this country, so he was especially proud of the professional paths Phil and I had chosen. My dad died in 2004, after a three-year battle with ALS—a tough way to go for anyone, but especially for someone who was so used to doing things for others, rather than having to rely on others to do things for him. Yet he never complained, and he never lost his sense of humor. It takes a lot of perseverance to write a book. Most of what I've learned about perseverance, I learned from my dad.

It also takes a certain amount of sacrifice, and the example there was set by my mom. We didn't have a typewriter when I was in school, so over the years she spent innumerable lunch hours, and countless hours after work, at her office, typing up my term papers, essays, and other writing assignments. She never even graduated from high school, but somehow her accuracy as a spellchecker was unmatched. I don't know that I fully appreciated how much support she lent to my writing at the time. I do now.

Support has come from many other quarters, as well. I'm especially grateful to our friends in the Bahá'í communities of Worcester and Sturbridge, Massachusetts, whose encouragement throughout the writing of this book has been uplifting and ceaseless. My four kids have been supportive in more ways than even they realize, not least of which has been the way they make me laugh. But it's my beautiful wife, Ardith, who has always been most supportive of all, whether I deserved it or not. I found truthfulness—the foundation of all virtues—when I found her.

# INDEX

||||||||||||

# ABOUT THE AUTHORS AND WRITER

||||||||||||||||||||||||

## THE AUTHORS

Philip Houston, Michael Floyd, Susan Carnicero, and Peter Romary are partners in QVerity (www.qverity.com), a company that provides training and consulting services worldwide in deception detection, critical interviewing, personnel screening, and elicitation techniques.

### Philip Houston

Phil is a nationally recognized authority on deception detection, critical interviewing, and elicitation. His twenty-five-year career with the Central Intelligence Agency was recognized with the award of the Career Intelligence Medal, highlighted by his service as a senior member of the Office of Security. In that capacity, he conducted thousands of interviews and interrogations for the CIA and other federal agencies, both as an investigator and as a polygraph examiner. He is credited with developing detection of deception and elicitation methodologies currently employed throughout the U.S. intelligence and federal law enforcement communities. The scope of Phil's work has covered criminal activity, personnel security, and key national security matters, including counterintelligence and counterterrorism. The fact that many of his interviews were conducted in foreign countries, coupled with six years of residence overseas, has given him unique insight and extensive experience in working with foreign cultures.

The story of Phil's success in creating a commercial application and market for the detection of deception methodology was featured in the 2010 book, *Broker, Trader, Lawyer, Spy* by Eamon Javers. Phil holds a BA in political science from East Carolina University in Greenville, North Carolina, and he is a 2013 recipient of the ECU Alumni Association's Outstanding Alumni Award. Phil lives with his wife, Debi, in Greenville.

## Michael Floyd

Michael provides training and consulting services for Forbes Top 10 families and large corporations throughout North America, Europe, and Asia. He is widely recognized as a leading authority on interviewing, detection of deception, and elicitation in cases involving criminal activity, personnel screening, and national security issues.

Michael is the founder of Advanced Polygraph Services, where he spent ten years conducting high-profile interviews and interrogations for law enforcement agencies, law firms, and private industry. He has most recently been involved in providing training and consulting services in the areas of detection of deception and information collection to firms in the financial services and audit communities.

Michael began his career as a commissioned officer in the U.S. Army Military Police, serving in the United States and Asia. He subsequently served with both the Central Intelligence

Agency and the National Security Agency. Throughout a career that has spanned more than thirty-five years, he has conducted more than eight thousand interviews and interrogations worldwide.

A graduate of the University of South Dakota with a BS in education, Michael also holds an MS degree in detection of deception from Reid College, and a JD degree from Seattle University School of Law. Michael and his wife, Estelita Marquez-Floyd, MD, live in Napa, California.

## Susan Carnicero

A former security specialist with the Central Intelligence Agency, Susan has twenty years of experience in interviewing, interrogation, and polygraph examination, focused primarily on national security, employment, and criminal issues. Susan is the developer of a behavioral screening program currently used within the federal government and in a variety of private industries. She is widely considered a leading authority on interviewing, detection of deception, and elicitation.

Susan has extensive experience in conducting training for federal government agencies and the law enforcement community, as well as for financial services firms and other private sector companies. Most recently, she has been involved in conducting high-level screening interviews within the U.S. government, and in providing consulting services for Forbes Top 10 families.

Prior to joining the CIA, Susan served in the investor relations and corporate communications field, where she achieved the position of director of public relations for a Fortune 500 company.

Susan holds a BA in communications from George Mason University in Fairfax, Virginia, and an MA in forensic psychology and MA in secondary education/English from

Marymount University in Arlington, Virginia. She lives in Chantilly, Virginia, with her daughter, Lauren, and son, Nicholas.

## Peter Romary

Peter Romary, a partner and general counsel at QVerity, is an attorney, arbitrator, mediator, and internationally recognized expert and trainer in the areas of negotiation, risk management, threat assessment and management, conflict resolution, and litigation risk management. He has provided consultancy services for government and private sector clients, and has lectured to audiences throughout the United States and abroad.

In 2002, Peter was recognized by the *National Law Journal* as one of the "Top 40 Trial Lawyers Under 40 Years Old" in the United States. He has been honored for his work in fourteen states, and has received the highest civilian honors awarded by several of those states. Among his other honors are the *National Law Journal* Pro Bono Award; the Ellis Island Medal of Honor; the American Police Hall of Fame Honor Award for Distinguished Public Service; and the National Crime Victim Bar Association Frank Carrington Champion of Civil Justice Award. In 2010, in recognition of his contributions to safety in higher education, Peter received the UNC Association of Student Governments John Sanders Award for Student Advocacy, the highest honor bestowed on behalf of the 215,000 students of the University of North Carolina system.

An adjunct professor at Campbell University School of Law, Peter holds law degrees from the University of Reading and the University of North Carolina at Chapel Hill. He lives in Greenville, North Carolina, with his wife, Marcy. They have a daughter, Elizabeth, who attends the University of Mississippi.

## THE WRITER

A veteran business/technology journalist and now a partner in QVerity, Don Tennant began his career with the National Security Agency as a research analyst covering international economic issues. His experience in producing key intelligence reports for senior U.S. policymakers prepared him for a venture into journalism, which led to his appointment as editor in chief of *Computerworld*, and later to the editorial directorship of *Computerworld* and *InfoWorld*. Don has conducted in-depth interviews with hundreds of top corporate executives and dozens of high-profile CEOs.

Don was presented with the 2007 Timothy White Award for Editorial Integrity by American Business Media, and he is a recipient of the prestigious Jesse H. Neal National Business Journalism Award for editorial excellence in news coverage. He has received several national gold awards for his editorial columns in *Computerworld*.

Don holds a BS in language (cum laude) from Georgetown University in Washington, D.C. He lives with his wife, Ardith, and daughter, Shelly, in Greenville, North Carolina. Follow him on Twitter: @dontennant.